Stortford Histories

'Snapshots' of Bishop's Stortford from Queen Victoria to Queen Elizabeth II

Mike James

Alex Andrijevic, David Clare, Sarah Stephens, Sarah Turner and Pam Williams

This is book *79* of a limited first edition of 400.

Published in Great Britain by the Bishop's Stortford Museum

Rhodes, 1–3 South Road, Bishop's Stortford, Hertfordshire CM23 3JG

www.rhodesbishopsstortford.org.uk/museum.php

ISBN 978-0-9571072-0-5

Printed by BPUK BookPrintingUK (www.bookprintinguk.com)

Biographies

Mike James moved to Bishop's Stortford in 1980 and has volunteered at the museum since January 2009. His interest in local history led to research in the County Archives and in the museum's collections to learn about the Victorian development of his Stortford neighbourhood, especially the individuals involved and their lives. Work with the museum's photographic and other collections, discussions with the staff and volunteers, and his own researches stimulated the idea of writing articles about the town's history for the *Herts and Essex Observer,* and thence the production of this book.

Alex Andrijevic is the Deputy Curator at Bishop's Stortford Museum. As a part of her responsibilities she has been running the Oral History project for six years and she is in charge of the digitisation, preservation and use of recorded memories of the past for the Museum's Oral Archive. She also looks after the Fine Art Collection and was able to contribute towards the article about Cecil Rhodes and his portraits.

David Clare went to school locally and has been a volunteer since 2007. He first produced material for the 2009 Rhodes exhibition on the First World War, in particular on the war experiences of his pacifist headmaster Norman Monk-Jones, who first ignited his interest in this era. Since then David has been researching the First World War and its effect on Bishop's Stortford.

Sarah Stephens has been a volunteer with the museum since 2009 and over time has taken on the role of the museum's photographer. Her main involvement in the book was to supply images of objects from the collection which went alongside and complemented the stories contained in the book. There are many wonderful objects to choose from so it was no easy task.

Sarah Turner has been the Curator at Bishop's Stortford Museum since 2006. As curator she is responsible for the care of thousands of wonderful objects which relate to the history of Bishop's Stortford and surrounding areas. She is currently researching information on the effects of the First World War in the local community.

Pam Williams has been volunteering at the museum for four years. As a relative newcomer to the area she decided that working in the museum would provide an insight into the heritage and an appreciation of the town which has become her home. Whilst working in the archives and researching an article on the Royal Wedding last year she discovered many more fascinating documents and photos of Royal events in Bishop's Stortford, which made her smile, sometimes despair and brought the town alive.

Contents

Introduction

Queen Elizabeth II's Diamond Jubilee will be celebrated in June 2012 and the volunteers and staff at Bishop's Stortford Museum have put together a souvenir book to mark the occasion. The book looks back at how Bishop's Stortford has changed and developed between the reigns of our last Diamond Jubilee monarch, Queen Victoria and our current monarch Queen Elizabeth II.

It contains a series of articles, some first published in the *Herts and Essex Observer* between 2009 and 2011 and some written especially for this book, celebrating the curious and the wonderful, the surprising and the mundane of this town during the last two centuries. The text, coupled with detailed photographs of objects from the Bishop's Stortford Museum collection, photographs from archives around the region and individual family archives (to all of whom we are very grateful for permission to use the images), tell these intriguing stories. It is hoped it will be a valuable contribution to the history of the town, and a fitting celebration for Jubilee Year.

This will be the first of many such books to be published by the Museum, and it would not have been possible without the tireless efforts of the volunteers at the Bishop's Stortford Museum, to whom the credit must go for researching, writing and producing it. They have agreed that all proceeds from the book will go to supporting collections care at the museum (via the Rhodes Birthplace

Trust, registered charity no. 1090267) thus helping ensure the future of our fascinating collections.

Hopefully, too, this volume will stimulate past and present Stortford residents to contact the Museum (01279 651746, www.rhodesbishopsstortford.org.uk) with your stories, updates and mementos. Then we can extend and republish this book again in the future.

We hope you enjoy it.

Dr Sarah Turner
Curator, Bishop's Stortford Museum

An invitation to the children's Coronation Tea from Bishop's Stortford District Council

PART I
Jubilees and royal visits

1. Queen Victoria's Jubilees

Pam Williams

Royal events have always been an excuse for big celebrations in Bishop's Stortford and around the turn of the 20th century these opportunities appeared regularly.

Queen Victoria commemorated her Golden Jubilee in 1887 and then her Diamond Jubilee in 1897. Both were causes for days of celebrations for all sections of society in the town, young and old, rich and poor. The town wanted everyone to make it a time to remember.

Sunday 20 June 1897[1] was a day of formal celebrations for the Diamond Jubilee, with special church services of thanksgiving held across town and a parade of the Volunteer Fire Brigade and Lads' Brigade marching from North Street to St Michael's Church for the morning service at 10:45 a.m.

Excitement began to build on Monday – invitations had been sent out in the previous weeks to 'the working classes and children of Bishop's Stortford', to attend the Old Court Room (in the Corn Exchange) on Monday 21 June between noon and 8 p.m. to receive gifts from Sir Walter Gilbey. For the chosen adults there were four different gifts: 160 handsome silver-lined copper bowls and a silver spoon; 160 white-metal tobacco boxes; 250 Jubilee canisters containing 1lb of tea; and 150 fancy canisters with ½lb tobacco and a briar pipe. Sir Walter also provided 1,600 Jubilee sixpences to be distributed to every child who attended the tea at Silver Leys the following day.

From a different fund the elderly and those on parish relief were given tickets for groceries ranging from

Above: Decorations are in place for Queen Victoria's Golden Jubilee celebrations in Market Square (1887).

Above: The Diamond Jubilee crowd and the parade (1897) in North Street, photographed from the balcony of the Corn Exchange. The rain kept off and everybody wore their 'Sunday Best'.

3s 6d for a widow or widower to 5 shillings for the sick or very poor, with married couples receiving more.

'Grinning through horses' collars' was just one of the competitions held on Monday evening at the Anchor Wharf in South Street. The Town Band played whilst the residents bobbed for oranges, had swimming races in the river and ran sack races. W. Knight won a pig that he managed to release after walking along a greasy pole over the river. Balloons were released into the air and the evening culminated with dancing to the band.

I. Jubilees and royal visits

Tuesday was Jubilee Day. It started with a bang at 6 a.m. – 20 small explosives were fired in the Town Meads (near Sworder's Field), followed at 8 a.m. by a Jubilee peal of bells at St Michael's Church. At 9 a.m. 'C' Company of the 1st Herts Rifle Volunteers marched from North Street via South Street and Hockerill to the Town Meads and ended with three cheers for the Queen.

Meanwhile, the population was gathering for a parade of decorated vehicles and bicycles. A total of 17 vehicles and 40 decorated bicycles with their owners in fancy dress were judged and then paraded through town. First prize (a pair of silver candlesticks) was awarded to Mrs Frank Flinn accompanied by her daughter dressed in white. They drove a small mail-phaeton decorated in roses, carnations and cornflowers with the motto 'Well played – 60 – not out'. Mr M. Sparrow won the silver cup for the men's bicycle class, dressed as Lord Nelson with his bicycle as HMS Victory.

In the afternoon it was the turn of the children to parade: 1,600 of them aged between 3 and 13 marched with the band from the town to Silver Leys for the afternoon sports and tea. There were flat races, obstacle races, three-legged races and tugs of war. The band race (in which the competitor had to play an instrument whilst running) was won by the drummer closely followed by the bugler. The greasy pole competition was not so successful as it was found to be too greasy. Eventually, when no one had managed to clamber even halfway up, it was abandoned and the prize money of 7s 6d was divided equally between the five competitors. After saying grace and singing the National Anthem, 1,584 children sat down for tea supervised by many women volunteers; they then repeated grace and the National Anthem at the end. Finally they were sent away with a Jubilee mug, a bun and an orange.

The evening continued with dancing at Silver Leys until 9 p.m., back to town to see the candlelight bicycle procession and then up to Claypits Farm (which was behind St Mary's School) on the Great Hadham Road for a bonfire at the end of what must have been an exhausting day.

The Poorhouse at Haymeads held their own celebrations the following weekend with lunch of Christmas fare: roast beef and vegetables, pastry and either beer or mineral water to drink. As each Christmas there was a debate by the governing board whether the Poorhouse inhabitants should be given alcohol, one assumes the same arguments occurred on this occasion! The weather was fine so tea was taken outside surrounded by bunting and fairy lights; the day finished with a concert including entertainers from London.

The permanent memorial of the Jubilee was to be a cedar sapling planted in Windhill. However, in case you are wondering whether you have seen it, 'permanent' in this case was reduced to just a few months as the sapling soon died.

2. King Edward VII: celebrations and visitation

Pam Williams

The sombre occasion of the death of Queen Victoria, a monarch who had reigned for 64 years and presided over huge changes in British life, was remembered by crowds in North Street who attended the proclamation of the new King Edward VII in February 1901. A large throng collected outside the council offices (now part of the NatWest Bank) as civic dignitaries read out the official announcement (*photograph below*). Edward's coronation was celebrated the following year with the usual parade, sports and an invitation to a children's tea. Sir Walter Gilbey supplied all the children with a book about the British Empire (*photograph right*).

Barratt's Store in North Street carried a stern banner: 'Righteousness exalteth a nation but sin is a reproach to any people', perhaps thinking of Edward VII's colourful past but Barratt's also wished 'Success to the Bishop's Stortford Flower Show' at the same time.[1]

Above: Book given to local children by Sir Walter Gilbey.

Left: The Proclamation of King Edward VII by town dignitaries outside the Council Offices in North Street; with mounted Police, the Fire Service and Scholars in attendance. The shop next door (now Oxfam) obviously provided a sought-after vantage point.

I. Jubilees and royal visits

Despite all the fervent royal support in Bishop's Stortford, rarely have we been visited by monarchs.

Edward VII came to Bishop's Stortford in 1905. Sir Walter Gilbey, who was a personal friend (horse-racing being a shared pleasure), managed to persuade the King to make a detour and drive through Harlow, Sawbridgeworth and the centre of Bishop's Stortford on 31 October 1905 on his way to Newmarket. The residents responded enthusiastically. It was reported that there was 'scarcely a lamp post between Harlow and Stansted that did not have some decoration or flag.'[2]

A huge 'Welcome' banner was strung across North Street from the George Hotel to Messrs Holland and Barrett on the opposite corner. An archway was formed by the fire escape ladders of the fire brigade for the royal car to drive under. Volunteers from 'C' company of the 1st Volunteer Brigade Bedfordshire Regiment, cadets from The High School and Fire Brigade members all lined the way in their brightly coloured uniforms and the Town Band played in Market Square.

However, all did not proceed as planned. Although Council members and town dignitaries were on their dais and Sir Walter Gilbey rushed into the road to greet the car there was some confusion and the King's car did not stop, he just carried on with his journey leaving everyone a little amazed and disappointed.

Left: King Edward VII's motor car drives along Potter Street.

Above: The King's car passes under the firemen's arch in North Street, so quickly that it leaves just a blur compared with the crowd waiting to welcome him. The vantage point above the shop beside the Council Offices was obviously popular (compare the picture of the King's proclamation on page 13).

Right: The massive crowd observed afterwards; carriages are trying to make their way back down the roadway.

3. Celebrations for George V and George VI

Pam Williams

Later celebrations included George V's coronation in 1911 (*photograph below*) with the usual children's treats. His Silver Jubilee took place just a year before his death in 1936. The jubilee was pursued with the usual enthusiasm with peals of bells and a town parade led by the British Legion band. At Silver Leys the band played on, and schoolchildren enjoyed a free roundabout and donkey rides; there was a musical clowns entertainment and Thurston's Funfair as well. Children's races (boys and girls) and a tea followed, with an inter-school tug-of-war competition (boys only, with 12 cricket balls and 12 cricket bats as prizes). The schools were St Michael's, Hockerill Boys School, Northgate School and St Joseph's School. For the adults there was dancing in the evening at the Great Hall (behind the Working Men's Club in South Street) and at Long's Hall in North Street; there was also a 'Social' at the Drill Hall in Market Place. Finally there was a bonfire at Silver Leys organised by the Boy Scouts, part of a chain of signal bonfires across the country.[1]

The celebrations of key events in George VI's reign were perhaps subdued, because of the nature of his accession, following the abdication of Edward VIII and then due to the hardships of the war years.

Changes in people's lives were reflected in the arrangements. The coronation of George VI and Queen Elizabeth was held on Wednesday 12 May 1937: free car parking was provided at Silver Leys, and at 11 a.m. there was a live radio broadcast in Castle Gardens of the ceremony taking place in Westminster Abbey. *Thompson's Mammoth Amusement Fair* had been set up at Silver Leys from Saturday to Wednesday.

Left: Bishop's Stortford celebrated King George V's coronation with a well attended parade on a bright day in June. This photograph shows the crowds in North Street. There were noticeably more motor vehicles in the parade of 1911.

The town's children were given a book of tickets (*photograph below*) for free rides on Coronation Day, on full-size or miniature roundabouts, a free donkey ride for the under sevens or a free pony ride for the over sevens. Variety entertainment was from farther afield, including 'Colorado and Lita', America's only lady cowboy act in Europe, with whips, cowgirl dances and lasso spinning. The day ended with fireworks as well as a bonfire.[2]

Above: Souvenir coronation medals were more magnificent than anything produced in later celebrations, reflecting the prosperity and optimism of the time.

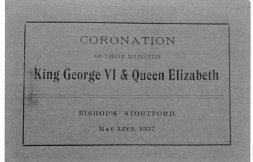

Left: Book of tickets for free rides for the town's children.

4. The new Elizabethan age

Pam Williams

Just 16 years after the coronation of George VI, his daughter Queen Elizabeth II celebrated her own coronation day. Although the King's death in 1952 was a mournful occasion, with 1,500 people collecting outside the Council Offices at Wharf House in the Causeway to hear the proclamation, the accession of Elizabeth II opened a new, post-war, optimistic Elizabethan age.

By the time of this coronation technology had progressed. At 10:30 a.m. television sets installed at Water Lane Institute (now the United Reformed Church Hall) and St Michael's Church Hall showed the ceremonies live from London. The town's sports and festivities were now held at Sworders Field. Teas and light refreshments were obtainable at the kiosk in the Castle Gardens; on Sworders Field a marquee provided beer and mineral water; there were also ices and sweets available. No expense was spared: there was a grand fancy dress parade (at 2.30 p.m.), displays of folk dancing,

children's sports, a riding display by *Syd Buster & his Cowboys*, Scottish dancing and puppet shows (3.00 – 4.30 p.m.). The exhausting day was rounded off by a grand torchlight procession (led by the band of the Bishop's Stortford Boys' Brigade), a 'Mammoth Bonfire' and ending with open-air dancing at Sworders Field (10.30 p.m. to midnight).[1]

Arrangements for the Queen's Silver Jubilee in 1977 were no less lavish than precedent demanded. It was memorably well-celebrated throughout the UK, with street parties, including in Bishop's Stortford (*see page 110*). The programme of events covered four days, from Saturday 4th June. It included an Elizabethan Feast (at the Green Man in Thorley – entry by ticket). Readers may recall it well. No doubt the current Queen's Diamond Jubilee (and Bank Holidays) on 4 – 5th June 2012 will be just as memorable for Stortfordians as her great-great-grandmother's was in 1897.

Above: The cover of a souvenir National Savings booklet, to encourage children (and their parents) to collect savings stamps.

Above: Souvenir programme for celebrations held in Bishop's Stortford to mark the coronation of Queen Elizabeth II.

Above: Commemorative souvenir to mark Bishop's Stortford's celebrations of Queen Elizabeth II's Silver Jubilee.

Traffic on the Station Road Bridge in the early 20th century

PART II

The Victorians and Edwardians

5. Coach travel and Stortford's inns

Mike James

Before the railway to London opened in 1842 and saw the abrupt demise of coach travel, coaches ran regularly to London via Sawbridgeworth, Harlow & Epping, and to Cambridge, Newmarket and beyond. By the Victorian era, following the improvements in road construction initiated by J.L. McAdam, the fast mail coach from London routinely took three hours,[1] a period when eleven coaches left for London on Mondays, the busiest day (*timetable below*)[2] nine coaches also went north, six from London. Before then the mail coach took about four hours in good conditions and weather.

We have few records of these trips. However, the style of travel probably differed little between the previous centuries and Victorian times. Fortunately, Samuel Pepys wrote

Right: 1839 coach timetable to London. Coaches from the George Hotel to the Bull Inn, Aldgate, were operated by Henry Gilbey, Sir Walter's father.[4]

entertainingly about coach travel and his experiences of Stortford (then variously spelled), including the hostelries where the many travellers broke their journeys in the 17th century.[3]

'[Monday, 7 Oct 1667] ...about nine o'clock, I, and my wife, and Willet [her maid], set out in a coach I have hired, with four horses... my wife and she in their morning gowns, very handsome and pretty, and to my great liking.'

They stopped in Enfield for lunch: '... it being but a foul, bad day' and then continued on:

'...and very merry, my wife and girle and I talking, and telling tales, and singing, and before night come to Bishop Stafford... and carried us to the Raynedeere where Mrs Aynsworth who lived heretofore at Cambridge, and

Coach name	Coming from	Stopping at	Departs
Royal Mail	Norwich	Crown Inn, Hockerill	2.30 am
Magnet	Norwich	Crown Inn	2.30 am
---	---	George Hotel	5.00 & 6.00 am Monday
---	---	George Hotel	8.00 am (not Sunday)
Times	Cambridge	Crown Inn	8.30 am (not Sunday)
---	Haverhill	Chequers Hotel	12.00 am (Mon, Wed, Fri)
Fly	Cambridge	Crown Inn	12.30 pm
Marquess Cornwallis	Bury St Edmunds	George Hotel	2.00 pm
Telegraph	Norwich	Cock Inn, Hockerill	3.00 pm
Hero	Fakenham & Swaffham	Crown Inn	5.15 pm (not Sunday)

whom I knew better than they think for, do live.'

The Reindeer Inn stood on the corner of High Street, opposite the George Hotel. Elizabeth Aynsworth was probably born locally: her father John Harrison was buried in Stortford. Her husband Edward was highway surveyor here, as was their son John. Mrs Aynsworth had previously lived in Cambridge, but was banished by the University authorities as a 'noted Procuress'. Later, it seems the University Vice-Chancellor and some

Above: Mr Robert Cole's house, the Reindeer Inn, in the 1880s.

of the college heads stayed at the Reindeer on their way to London and were entertained well, their supper being served off silver plate. The next morning their hostess refused any charge, saying that she was still indebted to the Vice-Chancellor who, by driving her out of Cambridge, had made her fortune.

Pepys continues:

'[Mrs Aynsworth] was the woman that, among other things, was great with my cozen Barnston, of Cottenham, and did use to sing to him, and did teach me 'Full forty times over,' a very lewd song [see p25]: a woman they are very well acquainted with, and is here what she was at Cambridge, and all the good fellows of the country come hither... but there was so much tearing company in the house, that we could not see my landlady; so I had no opportunity of renewing my old acquaintance with her, but here we slept very well'.

Mrs Aynsworth was in fact doubly notorious. On 10 September, just a month before Pepys's visit, William Boteler was hanged at Chelmsford Jail

Above: The site of the Reindeer Inn today, formerly Walkers & Co Provision Stores until the 1960s.

for the murder of Captain Wood of Battels, Manuden. Boteler and an accomplice had dined at the Reindeer. The night before the murder they had requested horses to be ready and then escaped. Wood had refused to loan money and been challenged to a duel. It appears he took this challenge lightly and went armed with his son's toy sword. One killer escaped to Holland, but Boteler was caught. Mrs Aynsworth was tried at the same time, as an accessory before the fact; on her way to the jail, in distress, she tried to jump into the river at Chelmsford Bridge. At the trial she was cleared for want of evidence.

Pepys and his party returned home to London from Brampton on 11 October via Stevenage and Barnett.

II. The Victorians and Edwardians

On 23 May 1668 Pepys made another trip, again stopping at the Reindeer:

> '[Saturday] Up by four o'clock; and, getting my things ready... I with my boy Tom... to the Bull, in Bishopsgate Street, and there, about six, took coach, he and I, and a gentleman and his man, there being another coach also, with as many more, I think, in it; and so away to Bishop's Stafford. Dined, and changed horses and coach, at Mrs. Aynsworth's: but I took no knowledge of her. ...Here I hear Mrs. Aynsworth is going to live at London: but I believe will be mistaken in it; for it will be found better for her to be chief where she is, than to have little to do at London. There being many finer than she there.'

Perhaps, in reality, she thought to escape her notoriety and seek anonymity in the capital? The journey was difficult:

> '...they had fair weather [at Newmarket] yesterday, though we here [at Stortford], and at London, had nothing but rain, insomuch that the ways are mighty full of water, so as hardly to be passed...

[Nevertheless] After dinner away again and come to Cambridge, after much bad way, about nine at night' [the trip taking about an hour longer].

At The Rose at Cambridge, exhausted:

> 'I met my father's horses, with a man, staying for me. But it is so late, and the waters so deep, that I durst not go to-night; but after supper to bed; and there lay very ill, by reason of some drunken scholars making a noise all night.'

Pepys returned through Stortford three days later but not to the Reindeer:

> '[At Cambridge] Up by four o'clock; and by the time we were ready, and had eat, we were called to the coach, where about six o'clock we set out... and so about noon [representing a normal trip] come to Bishop's Stafford, to another house than what we were at the other day, and better used. And here I paid for the reckoning 11s., we dining together, and pretty merry'.

In 1839 this coach would have stopped at the Crown, Hockerill, which was a major coaching hostelry.

Towards London road conditions remained bad:

> 'and then set out again, sleeping most part of the way; and got to Bishopsgate Street before eight o'clock, the waters being now most of them down... and we avoiding the bad way in [Epping] forest by a privy way, which brought us to Hodsden.'

Despite her notoriety, Mrs Aynsworth remained at the Reindeer. It was leased in the 1680s by John Aynsworth when she supplied refreshment to St Michaels for visiting preachers. She was buried at St Michael's 22 March 1686.

By Victorian times the hostelries in Stortford may have become more sedate; but, perhaps like today, Saturday nights remained boisterous. The railway's advent ended long-distance horse-powered transport which had been in existence for millennia. Horse-drawn traffic however, which took train passengers to and from the station flourished and was regularly seen collecting passengers outside the George Hotel, North Street.

Based on an article by Nancy Poole.[5]

The words of *Full Forty Times Over*[6]

(having a naval thrust appropriate to Pepys who was Secretary to the Admiralty)

Full forty times over I have strived to win,
    Full forty times over repulsed have been,
    But 'tis forty to one but I'll tempt her agen:
    For he's a dull Lover,
    That so will give over,
    Since thus runs the sport,
    Since thus runs the sport.
    Assault her but often, and you carry the Fort,
    Since thus runs the sport,
    Assault her but often, and you carry the Fort.

There's a breach ready made, which still open hath been,
    With thousands of thoughts to betray it within,
    If you once but approach you are sure to get in,
    Then stand not off coldly,
    But venter on boldly,
    With weapon in hand,
    With weapon in hand,
    If you once but approach, she's not able to stand,
    With weapon in hand:
    If you once but approach, she's not able to stand.

Some Lady-birds when down before them you sit,
    Will think to repulse you with Fire-balls of wit,
    But alas they'r but crackers, and seldome do hit;
    Then vanquish them after,
    With alarms of laughter,
    Their Forces being broke,
    Their Forces being broke,
    And the fire quite out, you may vanquish in smoak;
    Their Forces being broke,
    And the fire quite out, you may vanquish in smoak.

With pride & with state, some out-works they make,
    And with Volleys of frowns drive the enemy back:
    If you mind her discreetly she's easie to take,
    Then to it, ne'r fear her,
    But boldly come near her,
    By working about,
    By working about:
    If you once but approach, she can ne'r hold it out,
    By working about,
    If you once but approach, she can ne'r hold it out.

Some Ladies with blushes and modesty fight,
    And with their own fears the rude foe do affright,
    But they'r eas'ly surpriz'd if you come in the night;
    Then this you must drive at,
    To parley in private,
    And then they're o'rthrown,
    And then they'r o'rthrown,
    If you promise them farely, they'l soon be your own,
    And then they'r o'rthrown,
    If you promise them fairly, they'l soon be your own.

6. Commerce wins over the old King's Head

Mike James

The Corn Exchange, built in 1828, replaced the King's Head Inn in Market Square (*see images opposite*). Designed by Lewis Vulliamy it contained meeting rooms and the Magistrates' Court; its fashionable Classical style was an unambiguous statement of municipal wealth. Although many of its functions gradually moved into larger, purpose-made premises in the Victorian era (for example, the Working Men's Club in South Street provided meeting rooms), it remained in active commercial use well into the 20th century.

Part of the drive to construct the Corn Exchange was motivated by increased trade opportunities brought to Bishop's Stortford by the Stort Navigation. Opened nearly 60 years before, it had provided a highway from Stortford to London, then the largest city in the world, for the delivery of grain and malted barley. Before the age of clean water, beer was preferred so London provided an unquenchable market.

In 1828 Mullinger of North Street (later Boardmans, now the *Observer*) printed a 30-page *Abstract of the Title to the Corn Exchange ... and Copy of the Conveyance from Mr George Perry to the Trustees.*[1] Fifty-nine Trustees subscribed for 60 shares in the Corn Exchange company to buy 'The Old Kings Head with all the yards, stables, Haylofts, edifices and buildings thereunto... also all those several tenements, shops, sheds and stables...'

The Abstract is a long, circumlocutious document – a lawyer's masterpiece. Before today's Land Registry, precious individual deeds, handscripted on vellum for posterity, had to be physically located, examined and listed. All property owners had their strong boxes to keep their documents safe.

Perry received £3,150 (approximately £31,000 in today's currency), small beer for a prime location today but then about 120 times the annual agricultural wage.

The Trustees included eleven maltsters, nine gentlemen (mostly lawyers), eight brewers, six farmers and esquires (i.e. landowners), four bankers, four millers, and other traders. Seven were from London (mostly brewers) and three from Cambridgeshire, but the great majority were from the local area.

Among them Cheffins (Builder and Gentleman) is a name familiar today, but the partners in Hawkes Brewery (then in Water Lane) F.J. Nash and R. Jennings are mostly unremembered. J.H. Summers, Ironmonger, owned a shop on North Street (now part of Pearsons); as an auctioneer he was already cornering town sales (including share sales). Sir George Duckett, Baronet, nephew of Sir George Jackson (the Navigation's promoter, remembered in the name Jackson Square) purchased two shares. C.F. Foster, Merchant, was a partner in Fosters' Bank, Cambridge.[2] G. Perry, Innkeeper, also bought in – clearly appreciating a good deal when he saw one.

Left: A 19th century print showing the King's Head Inn sold by George Perry to make way for the Corn Exchange in 1828. The building in the right foreground is the George Hotel. The sign of the Bell Inn to the left is also visible.

Left: A 19th century print showing the Corn Exchange in 1842 when the building had become a business and community centre, housing meeting rooms, the Exchange and a Magistrate's Court (but not yet a bank). The building in the left background of this print and the one above was the Plume of Feathers public house, now Baroosh.

7. Fighting crime and the new model police station

Mike James

In 1886 designs for new model purpose –built police stations were first published by Sir Edmund Du Cane, Surveyor-General of Prisons. Plans included courtrooms, offices for the Superintendent, his lodgings, stabling yards with access to the cells, a kitchen for the officers, sanitary arrangements and gas lighting.[1]

For the police in Bishop's Stortford new quarters were overdue. In 1868 the old Church Street station had accommodated Superintendent Ryder and eleven other officers (*photograph next page*) who were responsible for a manor encompassing Stortford, Albury, Furneaux Pelham, Little Hadham and Sawbridgeworth. The Stortford station was condemned in the 1880s as unfit for human habitation. Urban Smith, the splendidly named Hertfordshire County Surveyor, designed a replacement based on the new model. He built similar stations in Hatfield, Hertford, Royston and Watford around the same time. In Bishop's Stortford the new station opened in 1890. The cells were downstairs. Inmates recorded their stay in graffiti: 'Turk 5 days', 'Lou 130 days hard labour', 'Gus Curtis knocked off Aug 1st 1927' and, poignantly, 'Gus Curtis same old tale'.

Stortford, though peaceable, had its share of incidents. In April 1889 Mr A. S. Barrett of Chantry Villa (proprietor of Holland & Barrett's Store, 4 North Street) reported the loss of a nest of 20 turkey eggs.[2] More seriously, about the same time, a former pupil and frequent truant of the British School (Northgate End) had been arrested for molesting a young lady in Cricketfield Lane. At that time, traffic accidents were horse-related: in November 1886 two children, Annie Knight and Florence Newman, were knocked down outside the school by a runaway horse.[3] Town parades, then as now, attracted large crowds, but the police presence was usually inconspicuous.

The man in charge at this time was Superintendent Spriggs (*photograph*

Above: Superintendant Spriggs

above). He wished to retire in 1914 but was asked to stay on after the start of the First World War. His sons Ernie, Bill and Ruben enlisted in the armed forces: Bill was killed in action in 1916 and Ernie died in 1921 in Sierra Leone, possibly from lung injuries received during the war.

The town eventually outgrew its model police station. The new station and Magistrates' Court was opened in Basbow Lane in 1940.

With thanks to Sarah Turner.

Right: The Stortford force in 1888. From left to right the officers are Gardiner, House, Parish, Shepherd, York, Newland, Ryder, Monk, Gatwood, Bryce, Platt and Whackett. Superintendant Ryder is centre front; the tall hats and whiskers added presence.

Credit: Hertfordshire Archives and Local Studies (HALS).

Left: The old police station and courthouse in Church Street today; access to the cells was via a gated entrance further up the street.

Right: Superintendent Spriggs with his family at the station c. 1910.

Credit: The Spriggs family images are courtesy of Mrs Helen Wright.

8. Stortford's police record is a good one

Mike James

When the former police station in Church Street was renovated in 1996 a rare collection of police records was discovered in its loft. It complements another collection left anonymously at Harlow Museum, and then deposited at Hertfordshire Archives and Local Studies (HALS) in 1992. Altogether, some 120 volumes include occurrence and attendance books, constables' journals, receipt books, charge sheets and bail documents covering the years 1841 (when the Hertfordshire Constabulary was formed) to 1919. It is one of the most complete records in the country, covering the early history of the force until it was regularised in late Victorian times.

Whether or not the officers realised what an interesting social record they had compiled, they saved it in the attic. The storage conditions, however, were imperfect so much conservation work is required, especially on the older ledgers.

The attendance books were purpose-made ledgers of alternately bound pages of writing paper and pink blotting-paper.

The records provide fascinating insights into the daily routine of the local police. Local beats included Church Street to Northgate End, to 'the Bridge' (possibly in Bridge Street?), back to Northgate End then the Station. Many beats in 1910 must have been bicycled: Albury at 3.30 p.m. to Furneux Pelham Hall, then Gravesend for 2 a.m.

Enquiries to the police were extremely varied: to find two servant girls who had run away from St Albans; a black cow from Havers Farm last seen in Rye Street; money stolen from a public house in Redbourn; a hat box lost from a motor car between Sandringham and Royston – 'please return to Buckingham Palace.'

With thanks to Nick Connell (HALS) and Sarah Turner.

Left: Attendance ledger, 1888, shows the ravages of damp, mould and acid decay. Two entries at the bottom left read 'Confer with Supt Innes re rabbits stolen'; many entries simply indicate duty at the Fire Station, stables or town.

Right: Receipts for lost and found items, prisoners' meal tickets and bills from the police record collection, with spike holes (the dark stain) and the original spike.

The Constables' Occurrence Books, in good handwriting but idiosyncratic syntax and spelling, record thousands of daily mini-dramas in breathless style:

> **(1888)** I was on duty in North Street 1 p.m. when my attention was drawn to a crowd of People standing in front of the Eagle Public House [at Half Acres and Hadham Rd] I proceeded to the spot and found that a collision had taken place, Between a bakers cart belonging to Mr F. Glasscock, baker, South Street Bps Stortford, and a wagon belonging to Mr John Pattern, farmer, Gt Hormead Herts, the man in charge of Mr Pattern's wagon went in the Eagle Public House to borrow a pale to give his horses some water, the time he was away Mr Glasscock's baker drove up with his cart and stopped close by, when he started on again Mr Pattern's horses started too, and ran the wagon shaft into the side of Mr Glasscock's cart, and threw horse, cart and man all over, but neither horse or man where injured, the only damage done was one shaft broke and part of one side of Mr Glasscock's cart. I reported the particulars to Mr Glasscock, and he said he should expect Mr Pattern to pay damages

II. The Victorians and Edwardians

more examples of Occurrence Book entries ...

(1901) Mr Bradfield reported ... that some children having a rope across the road & foot path in the New Town Road, which triped him up, as he was walking down the road thereby scratching his hands and face but was unable to find out who they were & wishes the Police would interfere.

(1902) Mr Hickmoss ... complains ... that about 11.20 a.m. today he was driving his pony & cart along the Thorley road & a motor car met him & frightened his pony, & the trap turned over & through his wife and himself & a friend onto the bank & his little daughter was thrown out so the cart wheel ran over her, but only Mrs Hickmoss was hurt she having a sprained Anckle. His cart is smashed the motor car never stopped & Mrs Hickmoss said it was travelling at 25 miles an hour the motor was carraying 3 men & was painted slate & light Chocolate colour that is all the discription he can give. I went up to the Railway Hotel & saw a Motor Car which came from that way carraying 2 men but Mr Hickmoss said it was not the one.

(1903) About 9.50 p.m. I was on duty in Potter Street when I saw a man named James Little of Hadham Rd Standing in the road & George Carter Holding him up. I heard him shouting out as he was in pain, I sat him on a chair & went & got the Police Stretcher & took him home with the help of some men, & removed his artificial leg & then felt that he had fractured his hip Bone & Doctor Hartley saw him, & ordered his removal to the hospital, and removed him there with the assistance of Serg 136 & PC 231.

and, responding to First World War fears ...

(1915) Suspected Spy. 10.30 p.m. Albert Puttick, Caretaker of the Liberal Club, Bishops Stortford, reports that ... About 5.30 pm while walking along Hallingbury Road, near the Garden fields he saw a man looking down towards the Rly line, and By his mannor & actions, Puttick thinks he was spying. This man disappeared some where, He cannot say as to what way he went. But thought he went down Across the field to the line. Description Age about 25 to 30 height 5 9 or 10. Dark Brown suit & Cap rather dark appearance.

Above: A force to respect – the Stortford Constabulary in 1912; The Superintendent is centre front. It seems beards were out of favour by then, but moustaches were in.

Credit: HALS (ref ACC 2630).

Scrumping!

A receipt signed by C. L. White in September 1901 acknowledging the safe return of his pear.

The hole in the centre of this receipt is from the spike (*see photograph on page 31*) on which the receipt was kept. There are hundreds of receipts in the police records and many other loose documents too. Receipts like this one include subjects as wide as lost-and-found items, meal receipts for the cost of feeding prisoners, the personal property of suicide victims, equipment receipts including the acknowledgement of receiving police uniforms by the officers. They provide insight into many aspects of the Victorian police force's duties.

HERTS CONSTABULARY.

B or Bp⁰ Stortford Division.

No. 1190

No. of Charge _____ 28ᵗʰ Sept _____ 1901

Received from Supt Foster

the following property : Cash _____

Other Articles :

One Pear stolen from My Garden.

C. L. White

Witness _____

9. The astonishing story of John Dobede Fairman

Mike James

Above: Photograph of North Street c. 1900 showing the White Hart over the entrance to Holland and Barrett's shop. It is now situated a few shops further up the street, above White Stuff, formerly Boardmans.

The White Hart was the emblem of the 1st Herts Light Horse Volunteer Cavalry, who were based at Silver Leys, Hadham Road.

There were many such volunteer forces formed to protect the realm after the Napoleonic wars. John Dobede Fairman, a wealthy maltster of Bishop's Stortford, formed, captained and largely financed the new 1st Herts Cavalry in November 1862, having previously been an officer in the West Essex Yeomanry Cavalry.[1] By all accounts (many in the

John Dobede Fairman (1823–1907), Captain-Commandant of the 1st Herts Cavalry, Director of the Bishop's Stortford, Dunmow & Braintree Railway Co. maltster, property owner, bachelor and then bankrupt. Credit: HALS (ref D/EL/1151).

Herts and Essex Observer) the 1st Herts was enormously successful. It was popular and recruited members who led it to great professional success. The 1st Herts gained considerable distinction at mounted sword drills in national competitions and inspections in the 1870s.

Their Silver Leys base was built by Fairman on his land; the club house on Windhill (now a private home) was also his property; he entertained the members to dinners and functions; he provided competition cups, memorabilia (photographs page 39) and weaponry: Bishop's Stortford Museum has a highly decorated sabre (see page 41) presented to Sergeant Major Cowell for 'regular attendance at drill': Cowell was a mainstay of the force including being Club Secretary.

In 1866 probably as a result of its successes, Fairman was appointed Captain-Commandant by Queen Victoria. Around this time Benjamin Lancelotte, a cavalry corporal from Backford, Cheshire about ten years Fairman's junior, was recruited. He was promoted to Captain of the 1st Herts in the 1870s. He lived next door to Fairman in Windhill.

Fairman owned malthouses and other property in Stortford. He (and his father before him) acted as agent to the London brewers Truman & Co. purchasing grain directly from farmers with cash advanced by Trumans and malting it on their behalf. He gradually began to purchase grain on credit through corn-factors, while still taking the brewer's money, using his cash flow to finance the 1st Herts as well as property purchases. By 1878 the 1st Herts was highly successful but Fairman's finances were desperately shaky. Even so, in August he bought at auction the Railway Hotel on Station Road (now converted into flats).

Then, in January 1879, Sworders the auctioneers made him bankrupt. The implosion was gigantic. It was discovered that Fairman and Lancelotte had fled abroad in December just before the crash. The contrast between Fairman's previous high standing and the success of the 1st Herts, and his shocking bankruptcy and flight with Lancelotte (a respected Captain who was not implicated in the debacle), stunned Stortford's community.

At the first creditors meeting at the Chequers Hotel (now Savills, North Street) 53 businesses, mostly local, were claimants. The largest were Truman & Co. owed £81,922 (approximately £7.5M at today's prices)[2] and Philip Chaplin, a Harlow brewer, owed £48,336 (£4.4M today). The debts totalled £137,468 altogether (£12.6M today).

Ironically, Sworder & Co. were owed the comparatively trivial sum of £184 14s.

In April 1879 a reward of £50 was

II. The Victorians and Edwardians

offered for Fairman's capture on a charge of fraud (*photograph right*). The 1st Herts was wound down: liabilities of £2,000 were funded by its members.

In a large sale in May, Fairman's property was sold for £15,114 (£1.4M today). Controversially, Truman & Co. seized all his barley and malt, worth £60,000 (approximately £5.5M). The creditors objected, arguing that Fairman bought it on his own account and therefore the proceeds belonged to them all. Truman & Co. counterclaimed that since Fairman, their agent, was advanced Truman money, the grain belonged to them. This argument passed through successive legal stages (which must have greatly dissipated the eventual gains) ascending eventually to the House of Lords. Truman & Co. finally won their case[3] in 1882.

We do not know where Fairman and Lancelotte fled. It seems unlikely that Fairman was eventually tried for fraud or imprisoned; but we do know that in September 1884 he resurfaced.

Nearly six years after their flight and two and a half years after the Truman and Co. case was finally settled, bankruptcy proceedings were restarted.

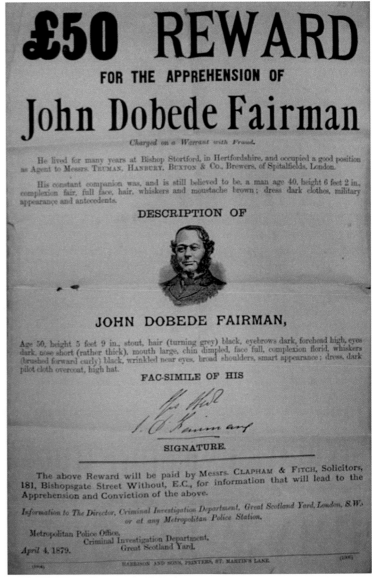

Above: Wanted notice issued by Scotland Yard.
Credit: HALS (ref D/EL/1151)

Fairman's public examination (the first he had attended) apparently proceeded quietly. The following January Fairman applied for his discharge from bankruptcy, which was finally granted on 12 February 1885, six years after his financial implosion and flight.

Lancelotte (Fairman's 'constant companion' according to the wanted notice) died on 7 April 1889 aged 56. He is recorded as a 'Gentleman' living near Abergele, Colwyn Bay, just a few miles from his birthplace and the seaport of Liverpool. His sole executor was John Dobede Fairman, of the same address. Fairman afterwards

lived with his sister in Hove; he died, still unmarried, in 1907.[4]

Fairman had a colourful life. He was wealthy, handsome and dashing; a well-regarded entrepreneur and cavalry officer. He lived in a masculine world of clubs, uniforms, swords, drills and entertainments. He eventually faced notoriety in straight-laced Victorian England and escaped to a new life.

With thanks to Sarah Turner.

Above: Close up detail of the tyg.

Above: Fine earthenware tyg (three-handled loving cup) of the 1st Herts Light Horse showing the designs of the three sides, from Bishop's Stortford Museum's collection. Measuring 19 cm tall and 16.5 cm in diameter it held nearly 7 pints – a serious drinking vessel.

Sabre of the 1st Herts Light Horse Volunteer Cavalry

This beautifully decorated (and costly) sabre was manufactured by Hamburger Rogers & Co., King Street, Covent Garden, London. It is engraved:

'Presented to Robert Cowell

by the Officers of the 1st Herts Light Horse Volunteers

for regular attendance at drill'.

Sergeant-Major Cowell was a mainstay of the force. It seems likely this gift was a symbol of the officers' appreciation.

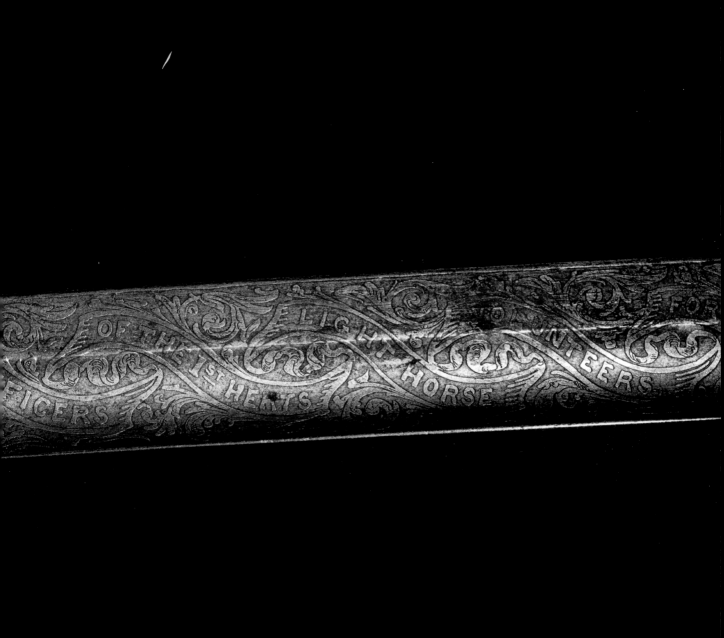

10. Chantry House and the man who built it

Mike James

Chantry House, one of the oldest former residences remaining in Bishop's Stortford, was built by George Starkins, now unremembered, but in his day a highly successful businessman and farmer.

In April 1823 Cockett & Nash of Royston designed the house for him at the Chantry. Although only a simple sketch (*opposite, top*), with just a few details indicated, it seems it sufficed for the builder. The sketch shows a handsome residence with large windows. It probably replaced an earlier Chantry building on the site.[1] Its appearance is identical with today's premises.

Inside it has been modernised: the original staircase may have been replaced but downstairs much of the decorative pargetting to the beams remains; upstairs there are large rooms and a finely panelled dressing room.

Starkins' father died in 1785 and left him (aged 20) a farm and the Windmill at Henham.[2] If his elder brother James had not died aged 17, the story might have been very different.

Starkins' business interests expanded: in 1796 he owned a curriers business (dressing, finishing and colouring tanned hide) and in 1811, a tannery (this business at Water Lane probably deriving from John Jones, his father-in-law). Property in Elsenham also came to him after his mother died (aged 92) in 1821.

Around 1826 Starkins formed his tannery business into a partnership with Frederick Chaplin,[3] son of the Congregational Church (now the United Reformed Church) minister the Reverend William Chaplin (to whom a memorial plaque still exists in the Water Lane church). Starkins may have been instrumental in inviting William Chaplin to Stortford in 1797 to take up this post. Starkins also acquired extensive farmland. An 1837 field-plan maps his 1,000 acres of farmland at Matching and High Laver. The 1839 tithe map of the parish shows he owned the 'Manse' and garden in Water Lane, which was then occupied by Frederick Chaplin. Starkins' death on Monday 23 January 1843 (aged 77), was recorded in *The Times*. He left 1,300 acres of Essex farmland, £7,500 of cash legacies (approximately £723,000 today), a beer house in Elsenham and 290 gallons of ale in his cellar.

His Will caused some drama. A map indicated how his holdings should be divided to provide income for his relatives and their descendants. Sworn testimony[4] records that on 24 January 1843, the day after his death, his Royston solicitors transmitted the Will to Chaplin (an executor) who read it over; he knew of the map's importance and so locked the door to the dressing room where it lay in a japanned deed box. After the funeral on 1 February the door was unlocked by the executors, the map was brought downstairs and examined by those gathered and the Will was read.

More drama occurred when it turned out that Starkins' birth was

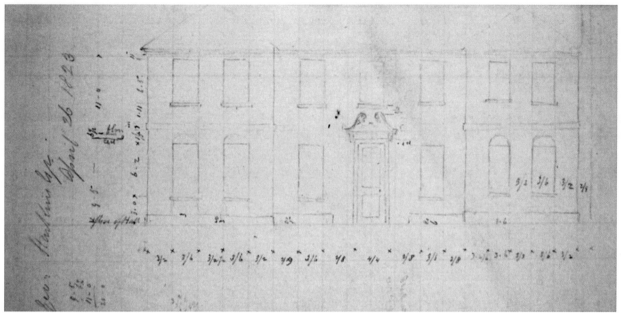

Above: Notebook of Messrs Cockett & Nash, Royston: sketch of dwelling house at Bishop's Stortford designed for George Starkins by Mr Savill, 26 April 1823. In the same notebook is an itemisation of the cost of the building dated 31 July.   Credit: Cambridgeshire Archives and Local Studies CALS (ref 296/B23; pp.1–2).

unrecorded. Fortunately his mother's Bible contained the necessary family detail and a niece was able to swear to the truth of it. Also, the Elsenham property had no deeds of ownership; however, a tenant testified that Starkins had owned it.[5]

Frederick Chaplin inherited the Chantry Estate and the tannery business. The house contents were mostly sold (also by Cockett & Nash), but not, it seems, the ale.

Left: Chantry House in 2009. The main doorway has been sealed and a new entrance created through one of the arched windows to the left.

Credit: Coke, Gearing for permitting interior access.

11. How local enterprise developed Bishop's Stortford

Mike James

Today we expect our taxes to fund services such as libraries, education, utilities and capital projects, but in the Victorian era of low taxes and small government such things were often paid for by local subscriptions.

In 1827 a committee formed itself to start a library in Stortford: 150 shares at £2 were sold, paying 5% interest annually through an annual membership fee of 1 guinea. Seven hundred volumes were bought initially and for over a century a room in J.M. Mullinger's house in North Street (later Boardmans, currently the *Observer*) housed the library.[1] The Corn Exchange was similarly financed and built the next year.

In 1859 a water works was opened by William Wilby at Mash Barns (now Maze Green Heights). In 1869 it became the Bishop's Stortford Water Co. permitted by Parliamentary Act to supply water for domestic consumption and sewerage; the working capital was 600 shares sold for £10 each.[2]

The Station Road Bridge is another example of local enterprise. Before its construction in 1865–7, traffic from the station area had to access South Street via Bridge Street. Pedestrians, though, could make use of a ferry boat service provided by Mr Newman.[3] Passenger access to South Street was made through Catherine Wheel Alley, which took its name from an old inn close by.

A new bridge was clearly seen as a great improvement because by February 1866, four months after construction started, 89 subscribers had raised all but £546 of the total cost of £2,665 (£0.25M in today's money). Land was both purchased and donated (total cost £600, or £56,400 today). There were 74 private and 15 commercial subscribers; donations ranged between £344 9s 6d and 10s. The Great Eastern Railway Co provided £150; most individuals gave 2 guineas or less, but the current value of that donation – £200 indicates their generosity.[4]

The bridge was designed (for £100) by George Perry, architect and son of the landlord of the old Kings Head Inn formerly on Market Square. Glasscocks, the builder, used a yard, now J. Day & Son Ltd, for their construction material.

The bridge abutments were strengthened by driving 30 piles of Baltic timber 22 feet long into the bank, and were tested using several tons of railway iron to make sure they could carry the load – empirical testing, not the theoretical, computer-assisted design that we know and love today.

Unlike the library or the Corn Exchange, funds were gifts – the return for the donor was the improvement in infrastructure we appreciate today. On 16 March 1867 the bridge and its approaches, having been completed and approved, were handed over to the Local Board free from debt. It is not recorded if Mr Newman the ferry boatman appreciated his enforced retirement.

Right: Station Road Bridge shortly after construction in 1867: the Glasscock team stands proudly on the far bank by their work.

Right: Station Bridge today: although the iron girders have been replaced and the abutments strengthened for modern traffic, it is clearly the same bridge.

12. How housing development has changed its style

Mike James

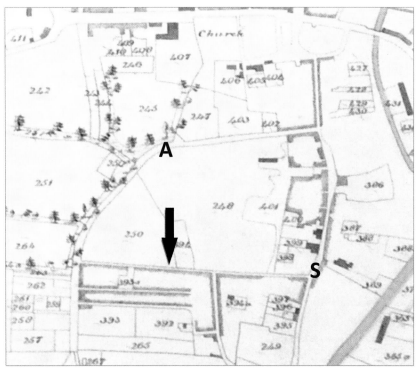

Above: Tithe map of 1839 showing the Newtown development (arrowed), south of fields bounded by Apton Road (A) and South Street (S).

Today, new housing mostly results from the activities of large-scale developers, but in earlier times development was piecemeal by private individuals.

In Stortford a first move towards estate housing occurred in the Newtown area.

The construction of the Stort Navigation in 1769 and introduction of the railway in the 1840s brought new trade and employment opportunities to the town, which in turn stimulated the development of new terraced rented housing along the south side of Newtown Road, in Castle Street, Middle Row, Back Row (now Oak Street) and Tuckers Row (the name giving a clue to the developer). Some of these houses still stand among later Victorian construction around the Newtown nucleus.

The trend for more uniform and utilitarian housing led to a surge in estate building across the country. Only in the last 30 or so years, in reaction, have housing styles been mixed up and greenery planted to improve the aesthetics of new estates. Yet there was a period in the mid 19th century when individualistic estate building was common: the Chantry Estate provides an interesting example.

The Chantry Estate arose because Frederick Chaplin (*see pages 42–43*) a Bishop's Stortford go-getter, spotted an opportunity. He realised both the economic importance of the railway to London and the fact that men who purchased land with an annual rental value of £2 could vote, a reflection of Chartist pressure.[1] He saw a new buyer's market of upwardly-aspiring voters, so the land was cleared and subdivided and a new access road (now Chantry Road) was constructed (compare the 1839 map and 1848 auction plan *below*). However, Chaplin was not to benefit because in the interim he was declared bankrupt. At the sale by Summers & Sworder for the Official Assignee, there were eleven initial buyers[2] who paid £5,865 altogether, but significant building was delayed, possibly because of a financial downturn, until the 1860s.

The first buildings went up in Pleasant Road (Lot 5) and the Chantry itself (Lot 1). George Pritchett, architect, then acquired much of Lots 5 – 7 and built Oak Hall (*pages 48–49*). Chantry Lodge (Lot 2), Emery Villa (Lot 3) and Rayments Forge (Lot 19) followed (*pages 84–85*).

The later influence of the post-war building boom can be observed at the north end of Chantry Road, built by Barrett's after the Pritchett estate was sold off in 1912. Nevertheless, the result, throughout Stortford, is lots of style and choice for the contemporary buyer.

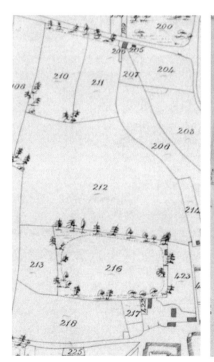 

Far left: Map of 1839 showing how the original field pattern controlled the Chantry development. The 'New Road' (later Chantry Road) was driven north from Hadham Road (bottom of map) along the boundary of field 217, across fields 216 ('Emery Field') and 212, then along the boundary between fields 210 ('Joslyn's Field') and 211 to Love or Deadwoman's (now Cricketfield) Lane.

Left: Summers & Sworder's auction plan of June 1848.

Credit: HALS (ref E583-604).

13. A Victorian 'Grand Design'

Mike James

In the 1860s the architect George Pritchett FRIBA, FSA (1824–1912) took three years to design and build Oak Hall, his home in the new Chantry Road. The fifth son of the Rev. C.R. Pritchett, Rector of Little Hallingbury, he was born at Charterhouse, London, where his father was a Reader. He was educated there and was, for 53 years, architect and surveyor to the Charterhouse estates of churches and farms.[1]

In 1849 he started a practice in North Street at premises replaced in 1889 by Hawkes & Co.'s brewery offices (now Edwards Interiors, see pages 58–59) which he designed. He designed or restored at least 62 local churches (including St Michaels Church, the first All Saints at Hockerill and Holy Trinity in South Street) as well as the Cemetery buildings in Apton Road and the present Saffron Building Society in Potter Street.

Pritchett was also an inventor and a collector of antiquities. Bells were installed using the new telephone system to call the firemen to the South Street fire station. He took out a patent for a central heating system in 1880. Knowledgeable about the new science of 'Roentgenology', he even acted as radiologist at the Rye Street Hospital.

Returning from his London office by train in 1865, he met Mr John Claydon who asked if he would like some good quality old oak from ancient school buildings built by Lady Bradbury of Littlebury. He paid £40 for the timber which was delivered and stacked in Joslyn's field.[2] Pritchett was then living in North Street. He already owned several acres adjacent to Joslyn's field (*pages 46–47*), the Oak

Above: Oak Hall, looking north-west from Chantry Road. Pritchett owned all the land downhill to Pleasant Road, being orchards and undeveloped fields. The view up Chantry Road to the house, now obscured by modern developments, must have been impressive.

Hall site, including cottages in Pleasant Road bought as a dowry[3] for his wife, Sophia Amelia, whom he had married the previous year.

The foundations were made of concrete and the raw materials were local. Pritchett also fabricated the bricks – part of his land had been a brick field – the brick kiln later made a store house (now a private home). Oak Hall remains an imposing two-gabled, three-storey, half-timbered building with heraldic mouldings in the façade; positioned face-on to Chantry Road, the roadway acted as a drive.

Pritchett furnished his house with antique furniture, fine oak panelling, Spanish leather work, porcelain, Old English stained glass, art, a large library, rare coins and archaeological curios (*pages 50–51*).

The June 1912 house sale following his death in February of that year lasted three days and contained 690 lots, including 'the fossilised tooth of an elephant found in Potter Street', secured for 10s for the County Museum at St Albans.[4]

The sale stimulated a suggestion from another antiquarian, the Reverend Dr A. Irving, Vicar of All Saints Church, that Bishop's Stortford should have its own museum, to retain and display such items of local interest.[5]

Based on an article by Nancy Poole.[6]

The south-west wing with heraldic mouldings representing (clockwise, from top left) Wales, Ireland, England and Scotland, a fleur de lys and gryphon (which closely resembles the emblem of the Midland Bank).

Above: Heraldic mouldings in situ.

George Pritchett's coat of arms and antique coin collection

George Pritchett's coat of arms (*above*), fixed to the red velvet lining of a box of antique coins (*right*), shows a gryphon (seen also in the pargetting on the outside of his house) and the motto 'Extra ne te quaesito', which may be translated as 'Nought beyond thy scrutiny'.

Besides being an architect (Pritchett was a Fellow of the Royal Institute of British Architects), the suffix FSA indicates he was also a Fellow of the Society of Antiquaries.

In the 1912 sale of Pritchett's effects, the box containing part of his collection of antique coins, now in the Museum's collection, was Lot 362. It was described as 'An old mahogany cabinet, covered in shark skin, fitted 12 trays with brass mounts, containing a collection of Roman silver and copper coins'. Lot 363 was another like it, but its whereabouts are unknown.

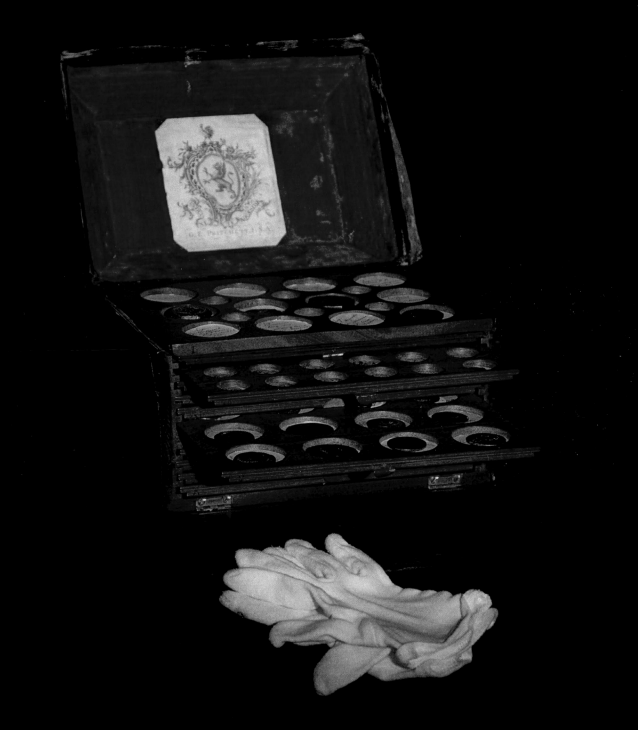

14. Selling your house in the 19th century

Mike James

In the centre of Bishop's Stortford today there are about eleven estate agents competing for your business. In the 19th century in Bishop's Stortford a single auctioneer supplied your needs (although there were other choices, such as Cockett & Nash of Royston).

In about 1820, James Hillatt Summers bought the auction business of Nathaniel S. Machin, operating from 17 North Street (then a coffee shop, now *Pearsons*).[1] Over time the firm evolved into Summers & Sworder, then it became Summers, Sworder & Summers, and finally it became G.E. Sworder & Sons, which still flourishes in Stansted Mountfichet.

George (G.E.) Sworder also sold ironmongery from his premises in North Street (*photograph opposite right*), so during financial downturns he had a safety net. Trade diversity was common then: for example carpenters were often also undertakers.

Property was then sold entirely by auction with the George Hotel (now Prezzo) and the Chequers Inn (Savills) providing the main sales venues. Many original Stortford sale details are preserved at the county archives in Hertford and Chelmsford; frequently a note of the purchaser and price was added to the details and important sales could include a plan as well as a description of the lots. These documents now provide fascinating insights into the area's development.

During 1886–91, for example, 138 'instructions' resulted in 55 separate sales covering 36 localities. Instructions for Stortford predominate (38%), but Stansted, Much Hadham and Sawbridgeworth also feature. Lettings, insurance policies, building materials, standing crops of hay, even shares (*photograph opposite right*) were offered, as well as agricultural and building land and dwellings.

Sales notices demanded attention: in 1848 the Chantry Estate (in 19 lots, see plan page 47) sought 'Capitalists and others to the sale of this truly Desirable Property, as affording the most favourable opportunity, either for occupation or Investment, that has ever occurred in this locality'. A seven-year mortgage for two thirds of the purchase money was available at 4.5%.

When the town was rapidly expanding in the mid-19th century, sales of 'tenements' were frequent, but later on 'cottages' were more common.

In 1889 no sales were held after July: the Great London Dock Strike (14 August to 15 September) involving 130,000 employees, perhaps unsettled the local market too much.

Business expansion was facilitated by the rail link to London. In 1848 potential commuters learned from sales notices that the train journey to London (Bishopsgate station) took 1 hour (the coach had taken 3–4 hours). In 1892 the train took 45 minutes to Liverpool Street station. Today, the journey time has decreased little more than 10 minutes.

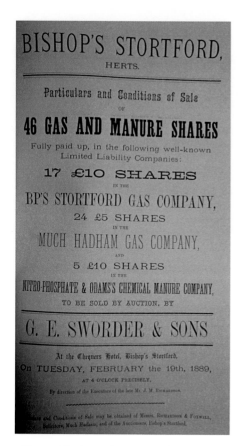

Above: George Sworder's ironmonger shop (now Pearsons) in North Street in the 1890s, where he also ran his auction business. He, his family and his staff, like so many other shopkeepers across the country, probably lived above the shop. Like many photographs of this age, it is showing signs of fatigue.

Above: Notice advertising the sale by Sworder's of shares. The sale was held at the Chequers Hotel, Tuesday 19 February 1889 at 4 o'clock precisely. The shares were part of the Estate of the late Mr J.M. Richardson.

Credit: G.E. Sworder & Sons Fine Art Auctioneers, Stansted Mountfichet, Essex CM24 8GE.

15. Family life in the town centre

Mike James

In the 1870s the population of Stortford was approximately 6,500 (today Sawbridgeworth's population is about 8,000). People lived close to their occupations in the town centre.

Two photographs illustrate how different life was then. The first (*photograph below*) shows the 'Manse' in Water Lane, with a family playing croquet, perhaps at a special occasion, in their garden (now Waitrose's car park). Owned by Hawkes & Co. the Manse housed their brewer Thomas Tyrrell for more than a decade.[1] The house and garden running down to the Stort (now under 'Old River Lane') must have been an attractive family residence.

Water Lane backs on to the former gardens of premises all along North Street. George Speechly, a chemist, had his pharmacy and home (formerly Boardmans, now White Stuff) here in the 1870–80s. Arthur Boardman (bookseller and stationer) and his family lived next door. The photo of Speechly's garden (*opposite page*) probably shows Amelia his wife (with the book) and their youngest daughter Carrie. In 1873 Amelia would have been 29 and Carrie aged 3. Based on resemblance, the other women could be Amelia's mother and sisters. In 1871 ten people lived there: George, Amelia and their three children, an assistant chemist, two apprentices (aged 17 and 16), a general servant (17) and a nursemaid (19). Although today the Speechly's garden has disappeared, the back of the building is little altered and the

Above: The 'Manse', Water Lane (now demolished) with the United Reformed Church behind. The croquet players are probably (L to R) Francis (Thomas's son, 19), Thomas Tyrrell (brewer, 60), Samuel (Thomas's eldest son, 32), Samuel's daughter and wife; c. 1875.

stables and a magnificent Ginkgo tree remain.

George Speechly hired an Italian sculptor to decorate the pharmacy's frontage:[2] he worked on the pavement to shape designs that incorporate botanical sources like poppy, fern, vine and foxglove still visible today.

One can still see the physical remains of these family homes and businesses, but what was life like for the families who lived in them? Did the Tyrrell, Speechly and Boardman families eat out as we do? The Trade Directories then contain no entries for restaurants, but there were many inns in the town: Market Square contained both the Curriers Arms (now Zizzi's) and the Old Bell (now part of Nockolds Solicitors) owned by Hawkes & Co. There were at least five hostelries in Bridge Street and High Street and four in North Street alone. Most of these would have provided food as well as drink, especially the George (which advertised itself as a 'Family Hotel') and the Chequers; they would have catered for an upmarket, family clientele, perhaps like the Speechly's and their visiting friends and family.

Above: The Speechly family c. 1873 enjoying the garden behind the pharmacy (now White Stuff). Tentative identifications are (left to right) Amelia's mother, Amelia Speechly, her daughter Carrie and two sisters.

16. If you want to get ahead, get a servant!

Mike James

Domestic Servants.

TO SERVANTS—DO YOU WANT A GOOD SITUATION? If so apply at once to the FREE Registry Office, opposite the Corn Exchange, Bishop's Stortford, where you can be suited immediately. Send stamp for reply.

WANTED—Good Cooks, £27 to £30, for Surrey, Harlow, Hoddesdon. Good Plain Cooks, £17 to £25 for Enfield, Woodford Green, Saffron Walden, Grays, Hoddesdon, Broxbourne, Enfield Lock. Cook Generals, £16 to £20, for South Hampstead, Stamford Hill, Hertford, West Kensington, Stanstead Abbotts, Highgate. Good Generals, excellent wages, for Upper Norwood, near Buntingford, Reading, Rickmansworth, Leigh-on-Sea, St. Margarets, Stoke Newington. Parlourmaids, good wages, for Surrey, Harlow, Chelsea. Good House-Parlourmaids, for Woodford Green, Enfield, Roydon, Harpenden, Much Hadham, Wanstead. Housemaids, £12 to £16, for Bishop's Stortford, Hertford, London, N. Kitchenmaid, £14 to £16, for Harlow.

TO LADIES,
DO YOU WANT A GOOD SERVANT?
The above office will be found an excellent medium for obtaining what you require.
Note the address : The Fancy Bazaar, opposite the Corn Exchange, Bishop's Stortford.

Above: Advert for domestic servants at the Free Registry Office opposite the Corn Exchange (*Herts and Essex Observer*, 6 February 1904).

In the UK in 1901 32% of females over the age of ten were in paid employment, the majority in domestic service.[1] So placing servants with households was a paying enterprise. There was a servants' Registry in Stortford which frequently advertised in the *Herts and Essex Observer*.

Servants were usually young women, domestic employment often being regarded as training for later married life. Employees and domestics commonly lived with their employers over the shop.

Albert Stubbing, born in Bishop's Stortford in 1861, was a grocer and provision merchant in Market Square (now F.J. Zelley, Palmers Lane) where he lived with his wife Sarah, their family and their employees. His sisters also ran a servants registry when they moved to Lowestoft (to 'The Wool Store' in Stortford House).[2]

Stubbing then had three employees living in: Ethel Welch (aged 16) grocers clerk from Dunmow; Herbert Kemp (aged 19) grocers assistant from

Above: The Stubbings shop (right, now Zelleys) in Palmers Lane on a wintry day c. 1880.

and dressmakers (men and women, all single, aged 17–32) all looked after by a housemaid/domestic and a cook.

Most domestic servants were usually from the local area even if the householder had come from afar, bringing some employees with them. A good example is Edward Agnew, Surgeon, 43, from Assam, India and his French wife Emilie, 31, from Paris. They lived in North Street with their three children who were born in Stortford. Their house-parlour maid was from Stebbing; but their cook/ domestic (aged 28) and nurse/ domestic (18) were from Berkshire and France, respectively.

With thanks to John Griggs.

Warwickshire; Harriet Phillips (aged 16) was the housemaid/domestic from Stortford. In most of the neighbouring businesses in Market Square, Bridge Street and Potter Street, including even the bank in North Street, the owner employed 'help'. Ellen Banks (aged 14), from Stansted, Clement Joscelyne's housemaid/domestic, must have been very busy taking care of his family of seven, while they looked after the store in Market Square.

Montagu Coates (Manager, London and National Bank in North Street, now NatWest), his wife and daughter, employed a cook/domestic, a housemaid and a nurse who, in their twenties, were probably more experienced and therefore better paid, indicating Mr Coates' status.[3]

Households must have been crowded. The premises of William Smith, general draper/shopkeeper, and Henry Laugher, outfitter/clothier, in Potter Street contained 19 people between them (7 family, 8 employees and 4 domestics). Nearby, Jane Inns, 35, ran a boarding house with 19 residents, mostly drapers assistants

Above: The rear of the former Stubbings shop in Devoils Lane, next to the Black Lion, with 'Stubbing Grocer' still visible on the gable end.

17. Messrs Hawkes & Co. are proud to announce …

Mike James

On 7 September 1889 the *Herts and Essex Observer* announced that 'Messrs Hawkes and Co. …will remove their office from the brewery yard to more commodious premises in North Street on Monday next'. The new premises (*see photograph opposite*), with electric light and telephone (now occupied by Edwards Interiors), was designed by George Pritchett, the architect (*see pages 48–51*). It was in Italianate style and built by the firm's own men under supervision. Stone dressing and carving were by Joseph Day (whose home at 100 South Street also has interesting decorative features) using Lincolnshire stone from the quarries of J. Houblon of Hallingbury Place. Carpentry (doors and counters) was by William Glasscock; plumbing by R. and J. Brazier; all were local businesses. Each room had a marble fireplace fitted with a stove surrounded by tiles featuring hops and chrysanthemums.

The stylish offices reflected a highly successful local industry. Stortford was an important staging post (*see page 22*) whose inns provided a ready market – with clean water taken for granted today we forget that beer used to be the universal, safe and nutritious beverage. Cereals and hops were available locally and barley malting was a key local industry. London was a prime market and the opening of the Stort Navigation and the railway (1842) significantly increased access to this enormous additional market.

In 1791 William Hawkes (brewer), William Woodham (farmer) and John Bird (maltster) had bought the Water Lane brewery from Hertford brewers John Fordham and Richard Flowers to form Hawkes & Co. It remained a family business, new partners often joining through marriage, until the death of Jones Gifford Nash (who lived in South Street) in 1876. The company expanded steadily: by 1830 it owned the Star, the George (now Prezzo), Chequers (Savills), the White Horse (Pizza Express), the Half Moon, the Currier's Arms (Zizzi) and the Dog's Head (in Market Place); strategically placed at Hockerill crossroads were the Red Lion (now the Crown Restaurant) and Coach & Horses. By the 1870s Hawkes had 66 pubs and 20 years later almost 200.[1] Their beer 'Entire' had a brilliant marketing slogan[2] (reminiscent of Heineken) since an 'entire' stallion has all its parts functioning.

Benskins bought the brewery and 161 properties in 1898 for £263,000 (nearly £24M today). Now, only the former offices on North Street and the walls in Water Lane (now the Charis Centre) and Water House (now Playsomething) conjure the brewery's former eminence (*photographs opposite*).

Brewing ceased there in 1916; the premises closed in 1987. The office building later housed the Midland Bank, which may have donated its gryphon to Mr Pritchett to embellish his house Oak Hall.

Based on an article by Nancy Poole.[3]

The 'Manse'

Water House

Left: The brewery viewed from the Meads (now approximately the Link Road) in c. 1879. Water House is obscured by the two-storey building (now replaced) indicated in the foreground. The scale of the brewery can be appreciated in this photo.

Water House

Left: The offices of Hawkes & Co. as the building is today, with a view of all that remains of the brewery. The brewery's brown stock-brick walls are evident; its entrance was beside Water House, just visible in the distance on the bend of Water Lane. The lane's brickwork still retains the scars of its encounters with the delivery wagons.

The maltings industry. The labourers in the photo below (c. 1906), taken just south of the Station Road bridge, work for H.A. & D. Taylor (Sawbridgeworth & Bishop's Stortford) and are loading sacks of barley into their warehouse (now the site of the Leisure Complex) for malting (an important driver of the town's prosperity). In 1901 Messrs Taylors were the main source of income for the Stort Navigation.

The beautifully-made brass chondrometer in the Museum's collection (*photograph opposite*), is shown in its hand-made, 30cm-long carrying case. It was convenient to assemble and was used as a desk-top instrument for measuring the weight of seed volumes using the calibrated brass bucket. The hardwood rod ('roll') was used to level the grain in the bucket correctly; then the measuring arm allowed the volume to be converted into weight.

Different grains vary in density, so a bushel (defined as 8 imperial gallons of water) of wheat weighs more (59 lbs) than a bushel of barley (47 lbs). In general, greater weight indicates better grain. But grain density also varies according to local climate, growing conditions and dryness, so a chondrometer was an important instrument to determine the quality of the product being sold. The lid contains instructions for use and a guide to measurement variation for wheat, rye, barley, oats, peas, small beans, Dutch clover, canary and rapeseed.

18. Cecil Rhodes and his portraits

Mike James

Bishop's Stortford Museum, at Rhodes, occupies two South Road semi-detached former residences, Thorleybourne House and Netteswell House. Cecil Rhodes was born in Netteswell House in 1853, the fifth son of the Reverend Francis Rhodes, the vicar of St Michael's. He attended the Bishop's Stortford Grammar School where he won some scholastic prizes, but Rhodes was not remembered there as an outstanding scholar.

Nevertheless, Rhodes' death, in 1902, aged just 49, was reported internationally. From relatively humble beginnings he had emphatically stamped his presence on the world. His death prompted the idea for a Memorial in Bishop's Stortford (recorded in the *Herts and Essex Observer*), finally realised in 1938 as the Rhodes Memorial Museum.

The Museum's art collection includes several portraits of Rhodes. The William Nicholson woodcut (*image opposite*) shows him 'dressed down', capturing his face exceptionally skilfully.

A very fine painting in the collection (*page 65*), the last of Rhodes, has just been restored. Painted by Philip Tennyson Cole at Groote Schuur, Rhodes' Cape Town residence, it was completed shortly before his death. It shows him in typically undemonstrative dress with shabby hat, but the face is particularly well done, especially his striking blue eyes.

Rhodes left his home town aged 17, to help his elder brother Herbert grow cotton in Natal, Southern Africa. The next year, after diamonds were discovered on land farmed by Diederik and Johannes De Beers, he began mining. Later, alternating mining in the English summer months with study in the winter months, he attended Oriel College, Oxford, gaining his degree in 1881. By 1888 he owned the entire diamond mining enterprise consolidated under the De Beers name.

By 1890 Rhodes was Prime Minister of the Cape. Apart from De Beers, he also headed the British South Africa Company with huge land interests including what is now Zambia (formerly North-Western & North-Eastern Rhodesia) and Zimbabwe (Southern Rhodesia), and ran the Gold Fields of South Africa. The Rhodes Scholarships at Oxford University were part of his legacy.

Rhodes was probably portrayed over 100 times, although he was never comfortable with portrait sittings. Tennyson Cole, having been forewarned of this problem, related in his autobiography[1] how, at their first session, after barely 20 minutes, Rhodes suddenly left. When asked where he had gone, his servant gave the stock reply "He's gone on his horse over the mountains". Nevertheless, Cole obtained further sittings, finished the painting and received from G.F. Watts, another eminent artist, great praise for its likeness.

Why then did Rhodes agree to so many portraits? A driven man, but conscious of his own mortality (he suffered heart disease from an early age), he was acutely aware that oil paintings were here to stay. Paintings engage, promote and advocate for the sitter. They build, through numerous brush strokes, bridges across time, influencing imagination and standpoint, forming a narrative. It is for us to interpret the story.

With thanks to Alex Andrijevic.

william Nicholson.

Cecil Rhodes.

Above: This woodcut portrait in the museum's collection is one of a series of seven by Nicholson commissioned and published in 1897 in *The New Review* by W.E. Henley. Others in this series include Queen Victoria, Sarah Bernhardt, Field Marshall Lord Roberts, James McNeill Whistler, Rudyard Kipling and Prince Bismarck. Such a range of individuals shows the considerable status that Rhodes had acquired by then.[2]

Portrait of Cecil Rhodes by Philip Tennyson Cole, completed 1902

Philip Tennyson Cole (c. 1862-1939) was a successful portrait painter, today hardly remembered. His autobiography *Vanity Varnished* tells the story of how this portrait came to be completed. It seems possible that Tennyson Cole painted the face from life, but completed the rest of the figure and backdrop afterwards – the hands and body, for example, appear a little too large compared with the head.

The arrangement differs from his other portraits of Rhodes. The surroundings are unspecific, but in the background the painting of Table Mountain is suggestive: an unusual backdrop, it includes Tennyson Cole's signature suggesting an actual painting is featured, although its whereabouts are now not known.

The pose is also very relaxed, hand clutching hat, suggesting Rhodes' restlessness, but hardly in dress appropriate for the South African climate. In other portraits Rhodes is usually shown with clasped hands, posed more stiffly. This portrait is illustrated in Tennyson Cole's book (suggesting it pleased him) but is there labelled *Cecil Rhodes, for Oriel College.* Oriel College, Oxford, possesses other Rhodes portraits by Cole.

This outstanding painting was recently restored thanks to an AIM/Pilgrim Trust conservation grant.

19. Costumes – what's in *your* attic?

Mike James

On Thursday 12 November 1903, Lady Victoria Kerr married Major William Gosling of Hassobury House, Farnham (afterwards Waterside School). Lady Victoria was a cousin of Queen Victoria; Major Gosling, of the Scots Guards, was a gold medallist at the

Above: The Edwardian society dress in the Bishop's Stortford Museum's collection.

1900 Paris Olympics, playing for Upton Park amateur football club to beat a French side 4–0. He was also an important local landowner and employer.

This dress, once owned by Lady Victoria, was donated to Bishop's Stortford Museum. It was thought to have been worn at her wedding. Being more than a century old, it required assessment and possible conservation, so expert advice[1] was sought from the costume curator at Colchester Museums.

Inspection showed the garment had a complex history of substantial alteration, its expensive fabrics were reused – not perhaps what you would expect of a 'society' lady. It was determined that this was probably not a wedding dress: its low front does not fit the high-necked Edwardian fashion; nor does the use of rich grey silk and gold thread brocade in the front panel of the skirt and the back, material which is much more typical of the 1880s. The

brocade has been supplemented at the back of the skirt with five panels of oyster-coloured heavy silk satin, longer at the back than the front. The collar, sleeves and decorative trim on the skirt are silk chiffon and lace. The sleeves are finished with black silk velvet ribbons decorated with bows and small diamante buckles.

The back of the boned bodice (*opposite photograph*) has eyeholes, indicating it was originally meant to be laced up, but later the centre back seam was hand-sewn together. The original wasp-waist typical of the Victorian era has been let out by adding pieces of brocade. The bodice and skirt have been relatively crudely sewn together and the skirt is, unusually, unlined. Yet the hand-work in the gathered silk chiffon trims is skilfully done. Was the dress altered to suit changes in style or had it been relegated to the attic and then reused as a costume piece for a theatrical production?

The dress was much worn: the hem is abraded and there are sweat stains under the arms with consequent damage to the silk chiffon. Perhaps it was a family heirloom thriftily altered for many uses during its life. Not only the poor make-do and mend.

Its survival and presentation to our Museum for everyone to enjoy provides a fascinating glimpse into Edwardian costume design and perhaps also the lives of Lady Victoria and her Major.

With thanks to Sarah Turner.

Right: The back of the dress, showing the richly brocaded gold-thread silk panels. The eye-holes are just visible, showing it was originally laced.

Advertisement from the *Herts and Essex Observer,* 19 August 1917, proudly promoting the employment of women in shops.

PART III

The First World War

20. Dad's Army 1914–18

David Clare

In the first week of the war (August 1914), Percy Harris, a London County Councillor, proposed in *The Times* the formation of evening camps for volunteers too old or unable to join the Army or Navy. Old soldiers would be used as instructors at these camps. Rather surprisingly this patriotic call greatly alarmed the authorities, mainly because it might interfere with recruitment for Lord Kitchener's 'New Army' by reducing volunteer numbers. Indeed, at the end of August the War Office banned such groups and their parades; circulars to Mayors and Chief Constables requested they remove any posters advertising such groups.

Percy Harris's persistence soon had the veto overturned and 'Volunteer Training Corps' (VTC) were accepted. The War Office agreed to provide only a red armlet showing a prominent 'GR', suggesting the volunteers' nickname of 'Gorgeous Wrecks'.[1]

Bishop's Stortford, at the suggestion of Mr R.L. Barclay, was the first town in Hertfordshire to raise such a Corp.

On 8 October, at a well-attended meeting at the Chequers Hotel in North Street, a committee was formed and Colonel C. Healey became Commander with Frank Kingdon and Ingram Daniel elected joint secretaries. There was a lively discussion about the proposed upper age limit of 60; it was decided that the routine route marches would quickly sort out that matter.[2]

Shortly afterwards the formation of Bishop's Stortford Volunteer Corps (BSVTC) was publicly announced. Men could enrol at the old Post Office (by Devoils Lane steps, part of the present Saffron Building Society premises) or at Mr Horabin's shop at 13 North Street.

Towards the end of October the first parade was held. Mr Barclay said their objectives were to keep things going, support His Majesty's Forces and to prepare for emergencies. The enrolment fee was 1 shilling. By the time of the second parade on 1 November it was clear that not everyone in town was appreciative.

Col. Healey told his troops 'it had come to his ears that some people were sneering at the idea of the Corps but that was simply like pouring water off a duck's back'. It appears such attitudes existed throughout the war.

In December 1914 the Army Council formed the Central Association of Volunteer Training Corps, under Lord Desborough; membership by VTCs became a legal necessity for recognition. The Army Council also required that a responsible officer, approved by the War Office, had to advise the group. No arms, ammunition or clothing would be supplied from public sources nor would any financial assistance be given. If the volunteers bought their own uniforms they had to be distinguishable from the Regular Army's. It was stressed that only those ineligible to join the Forces were allowed to become members. Thus the authorities only provided someone to tell the local volunteer groups what to do, and an armband each, but proudly announced that every man wearing that badge had the right under the Hague Convention to shoot at the enemy.

In December 1914 the *Herts and Essex Observer* advertised for volunteers for the BSVTC (*bottom right*). It was suggested that non-joiners would likely dig trenches or bury the dead. Even so, between October 1915 and November 1917 between 4 and 5 million man-hours were spent by Volunteer Corps digging trenches around London, with the BSVTC doing its fair share.

In March 1915 the 1st Hertfordshire (East Herts) Volunteer Regiment was formed; Battalion headquarters were at Bishop's Stortford. No. 1 Company, 1st Battalion, was the Bishop's Stortford and Sawbridgeworth Company (which also included Royston).

Each week the *Herts and Essex Observer* announced the Orders for the following week. BSVTC members had to attend 40 drills per year (each one hour in length), and attain 2nd class in musketry to qualify for an efficiency badge. Failure to attend twelve drills in six months led to 'resignation'. Members were not to be between the ages of 17 and 35 and the Corps was to be of a 'Democratic Nature' with members from all walks of life drilling together. Bank Holiday weeks were a particularly busy time (*see the table, below left*). We know the names of many BSVTC members, mainly organisers and men above the rank of private. G.S. Streeter took over from Col. Healey when the latter was made Commanding Officer of 1st Battalion. Streeter became one of only three members of the Hertfordshire Volunteer force to receive an honour at the war's end. The war brought no fatalities directly to the 1st Battalion, but one of its members was killed: Arthur Henry George Milton of 21 King Street tried to enlist in the 'New Army' aged just 16, but was rejected because of his youth; so he joined the BSVTC instead. When he reached 18 he joined the 26th Battalion Royal Fusiliers on 15 August 1917. He died of wounds on 26 October 1918, only days before the Armistice.[3]

Duties for the BSVTC, May 1915	
Sat. 22nd	2.30 pm: Musketry at the Great Hall 6.00 pm: Parade at the School
Sun. 23rd	2.30 pm: Parade at Mr Featherby's, South Mill, for route march to Walbury Dells
Mon. 24th	9.15 am: Parade at Railway Station; proceed by train to Hertford for Battalion drill at Balls Park. Each man to provide his own lunch
Tues. 25th	8.00 pm: Squad drill at the School
Wed. 26th	2.30 pm: Musketry at the Great Hall

Above: Bank holiday week rota for volunteers.

Above right: Recruiting for the BSVTC (*Herts and Essex Observer*, December 1914). The German fleet had shelled Hartlepool and Scarborough killing over 100 people. 'Remember Scarborough' was afterwards used on many recruiting posters.

21. Albert Ball, VC: a fighter pilot in Bishop's Stortford

David Clare

Above: South Street in 1915. Note the soldiers on horse-back in the background. The Anchor Inn was to the left; the 'new' Post Office (and recruiting office) on the right beside the Methodist Chapel is today the site of Tesco's Express Store.

Towards the end of 1914 Lord Kitchener's successful drive for 'New Army' recruits led to an unanticipated problem for the military authorities. There was not sufficient barrack space to accommodate all the new recruits, and with winter approaching the continued use of tents was not a viable option. So in the winter of 1914-1915 towns across the UK found themselves having to billet soldiers. One section of the army that was billeted in Bishop's Stortford was the North Midland Cyclist Corp and one of its officers was an 18 year-old 2nd Lieutenant called Albert Ball.

Albert Ball joined the army in his home town of Nottingham at the start of the war and was quickly promoted to Sergeant and then in October commissioned as an Officer. He had himself transferred to the North Midland Cyclist Corp in the hope it would see him drafted to France more quickly.[1] At that time he could not fly and it was only after leaving Bishop's Stortford that he decided to pay for private flying lessons at Hendon (*photograph opposite*).

While in Bishop's Stortford he was billeted at the Anchor Inn, 23 South Street, which was roughly opposite where the Methodist Church is today (*photograph left*). He was here until late March 1915 when he received orders to get ready for the Reserve and move to Luton. In a February letter to his father he wrote about how disappointed he was at not being sent to the front but had recently been told by his officer, Captain Black, that he would be in the first draft of reserves leaving in March. In this letter he also commented that 'Transport, troops, guns etc are rolling past in long lines all the time. It is very interesting. Ten thousand are leaving for France tonight.' Bishop's Stortford was exceptionally busy at that time.

Just before leaving Stortford he wrote to his father again indicating that he was not very happy, 'what with a death etc, I have had a rough time'. We now know the death he was referring to was that of Private George Harrison. He was with the North Midland Cyclist Corp and Albert Ball was his immediate Officer. Because of the nature of the death it was reported in great detail in the *Herts and Essex Observer*.[2]

Private Harrison was 27 at the time and until the morning of 13 March was billeted at the Anchor together with Albert Ball. On the morning of Saturday 13 March he left to go up to Mr Gerish's house, Ivy Lodge, at the top of Warwick Road, where he was to be billeted next. Later that evening he was with friends at the Railway Hotel where he ate supper and was drinking both beer and whisky. He did not appear drunk inside the hotel but when he walked outside into the fresh air his friends thought that it started to have some effect.

The following morning Dr Huxtable was called to Ivy Lodge. Arriving at 7.30 a.m. he found George Harrison lying dead on his mattress. Harrison had been sick in the night; tragically, his death was caused by asphyxia due to food in the larynx. At this stage Albert Ball would have been called in to take over arrangements for the body, coroner and funeral. He arranged a full military funeral for Private Harrison which took place on Wednesday 17 March at Bishop's Stortford's cemetery. A firing party from the Lincolns fired three volleys over the grave after which the 'Last Post' was sounded by the local Boys' Life Brigade Corps. Albert Ball laid his own wreath on the grave inscribed 'With sincere sympathy from Second Lieutenant A. Ball'. Private Harrison's gravestone can be seen there today.

Shortly afterwards Albert Ball left Bishop's Stortford. In January 1916 he completed his flying training, was awarded his wings, and officially seconded to the Royal Flying Corps. In February he was posted to France where he was killed in combat on 7 May 1917 aged just 20. During his time in France he became one of Britain's leading fighter Aces with a total of 44 aerial victories to his name, being promoted to Flight Commander. Albert Ball was decorated VC (posthumously), DSO and two Bars, and MC. At the request of his father his grave was left where he was buried by the Germans, in the German extension of the Annoeullin Communal Cemetery. Albert Ball's grave is still the only British grave there.

Above: 2nd Lieutenant Albert Ball at Hendon, 1915.

Credit: J.K. Williams
www.albertball.homestead.com/Gallery50.html

22. Oak Hall, the German Prisoner of War camp

David Clare

Oak Hall, George Pritchett's Elizabethan-style former home in Chantry Road (*pages 48–49*), was commandeered in early 1918 and converted into a Prisoner of War (PoW) camp housing German prisoners, mainly sailors. The land around the house had become a farm and this is where the prisoners, fit young men mostly, had been brought to work.[1] In March 1918 it is estimated that throughout the UK almost 9,000 prisoners were employed on farm work. Initially the Oak Hall prisoners were accommodated in the house itself but later in the year huts were erected in the grounds for their use.

The arrival of the PoWs in Bishop's Stortford created great interest among the townsfolk. A public footpath running through the grounds (which still exists, passing from Cricketfield Lane behind houses in Chantry Close) was a natural vantage point for the curious. However the actions of those using the path led to a public outcry, eventually reaching the National Press. On 21 July 1918 a Mr J. Bruce Payne was so outraged by what was happening that he wrote a letter of complaint to the Urban District Council.

Young girls using the path, it seems, were becoming very friendly with the young prisoners, giving them money, tobacco and cigarettes. He requested the Council screen the prisoners from public view because 'many of these prisoners are sailors and very possibly have taken part in the brutalities at sea which have shocked humanity'. The complaint was picked up by a Stortford sailor serving in the North Sea: he was disgusted by the girls' behaviour – why didn't they visit the local Voluntary Aid Detachment where our wounded soldiers and sailors were being treated?

The Council compromised and in July 1918 they closed the footpath to the public. The National Press disagreed with the action and suggested that, instead, these young ladies needed a good talking to from their mothers. The path remained closed but the prisoners could still be seen from Chantry Road; this led to a further letter from a Stortford resident in the *Evening Standard* on 24 August 1918, reflecting the population's gnawing post-war hardships: the writer complained that the prisoners were resident in a house that recently rented for £200 a year (more than £10,000 today) enjoying, by implication, luxurious conditions; and that cheese and fruit had been taken to the prisoners: 'cheese that I had forgotten as an eatable and looked upon as a luxury of pre war days'.

But such luxuries did not appeal to all the prisoners. Airman Wilhelm Drester (21) and submariners Hans Yost (25) and Franz Zitsel (24) were reported missing from Oak Hall around noon on Sunday 1 September 1918. A large manhunt was organised involving Special Constables and even the Boy Scouts. The prisoners were recaptured three days later, 45 miles away on Mersea Island. They had moved by night, following the Braintree railway line eastwards (parts of which are now a public footpath). When they reached Maldon they 'commandeered' an open boat and rowed twelve miles down the Blackwater hoping to cross the North Sea, but became stranded on the mud at West Edge, East Mersea. Exhausted they fell asleep and were spotted in the morning by a local farmer who called in the military: they were still wearing tunics with red patches that marked them out as PoWs. It seems they had excellent maps as well as plenty of food in their possession. By the Wednesday evening they were returned to the camp Commander, Lieutenant Gort, who also commanded PoW camps in Saffron Walden, Stansted and Standon. Sadly, Lieutenant Gort, who himself had been wounded at Gallipoli, died on 5 November, succumbing to the influenza pandemic sweeping the country.

Oak Hall camp remained newsworthy: in February 1919 Aaron Swan, a local baker, was charged with selling three loaves to a prisoner, who was in court to give evidence. Not only was it illegal to sell bread to prisoners but Swan also charged 1/6d for the loaves, which was over the legally set maximum. He was fined £10.

It is probable that the prisoners were repatriated mid 1919 as on 13 December the *Herts and Essex Observer* carried an advertisement: the Ministry of Munitions was offering for sale, through G.E. Sworder and Son, surplus equipment from Oak Hall. At a later auction the huts were also sold and Fishpools, the furniture retailers, bought at least one for storage purposes. The land then returned to its pre-war function as a farm.

Right: Oak Hall at the sale by Knight, Frank & Rutley after George Pritchett's death in 1912. The brochure, with photographs of the interior, conveys the quality of the property and why it might have rented for £200 p.a.

Went to France 1916

It is believed that these pressed flowers in Bishop's Stortford Museum's collection were taken to France in 1916 by Herbert Champness of Bishop's Stortford, or were acquired by him at the Front.

They arrived in the Museum in a small brown envelope with a handwritten ink note on it which says, poignantly, 'Went to France 1916'. The envelope is as much part of the object as the flowers and is therefore part of any consideration of conservation and care.

It is a miracle that the object has survived; the flowers are obviously a precious souvenir, but a small inconspicuous one that could easily have disappeared since 1916. They were stored with Champness's military papers, but beyond this information we know very little about him or the object. Herbert Champness survived the First World War but his brother, William John Champness, did not.

23. Women at war: the Land Army

Sarah Turner

On Wednesday 25 July 1917 Bishop's Stortford hosted what was advertised in the *Herts and Essex Observer* as 'the largest farming competition in the country'. About 5,000 people flocked to Whitehall Farm and Silver Leys, owned by Tresham Gilbey, to watch the competition and support the 340 competitors from across the UK as they competed to win prizes in categories ranging from milking, to hedge trimming, to carting manure.

The competition was organised by the Hertfordshire Women's Agricultural Council to demonstrate the skills of women farm workers and it was widely publicised.[1] It was even filmed to be shown in cinemas around the country and postcards were made of the event. *Pathé News* still has footage of the competition and Dane O'Coys Lane is clearly recognisable as women workers herd cows past the camera.[2]

The competition was an example of women's active involvement in the First World War. This was the Women's Land Army demonstrating its skills and raising morale on the home front.

A significant agricultural area, Bishop's Stortford saw a great number of women workers on farms. Initially some farmers had resisted the move to employ women in such a capacity; not so Mr Harry Cox, a well-known local man and farmer at

DEMONSTRATION OF
How Women are Solving the Food Problem.

HERTFORDSHIRE AND ESSEX WOMEN'S WAR AGRICULTURAL COMMITTEES.

WOMEN'S FARM COMPETITIONS

Open to all bona-fide Women Farm Workers in England, will be held

On WEDNESDAY, 25th JULY, at 3.0 p.m.,

At the WHITEHALL ESTATE, Bishop's Stortford,

By kind permission of TRESHAM GILBEY, Esq., J.P.

SUBJECTS FOR COMPETITION.

1. Milking.
2. Poultry Killing and Plucking.
3. Hoeing Roots.
4. Manure Carting. Fill load and set it out.
5. Hedge Trimming.
6. Harness Horse to Cart, put in and take out.
7. Harness Horse to Harrow and Drive one bout.
8. Driving Competition.

Prizes :—£1, 15s, 10s, in each class.

A SILVER CUP will be given to the Competitor gaining the greatest number of points during the day.

ALL ENTRIES ARE FREE. Forms of Entry and further particulars may be obtained from Mrs E. PAPE, Normanhurst, Windhill, Bishop's Stortford.

LAST DAY FOR RECEIVING ENTRIES :—Wednesday, 11th July, 1917.

Above: The Herts and Essex Observer 7 July 1917 advertises the approaching Women's Farm Competition at Silver Leys. The number of entries received compelled the organisers to move the start time forward from 3 p.m. to 11 a.m. Apart from cash prizes, silver cups were presented by the Marchioness of Salisbury for the best overall competitor (donated by Mrs Tresham Gilbey), the best Hertfordshire entrant (from A.S. Bowlby, JP, of Gilston Park, Harlow) and the best Essex entrant (from S.W. Robinson of Tye Hall Farm, Roxwell).

Havers Farm, Bishop's Stortford. He was one of the first in this part of the country to employ women farm workers and to advocate the important role they could play in agriculture. He was already training them for this work in early 1916, for which he received significant local recognition.[3]

By the end of 1917 there were over 260,000 women working on the land in Britain, including on local farms such as Claypits Farm, Hadham Road (*photograph below*).

Their work was vital to the war effort. By February 1916 Bishop's Stortford Town Council was discussing how to engage women on farm work and the need was becoming essential by 1917.

In February of that year German U-boats had sunk over 200 ships bringing food into the country; more and more men were being taken from farming and sent on active service. Farms needed labour and women took on these jobs and helped to feed the nation.

Working as part of the land army was only one of many jobs that women undertook on the Home Front in the First World War. Bishop's Stortford had a munitions factory at Featherby's, South Mill Road, which recruited many local women, including Edith Joscelyne (of the Clement Joscelyne family). There was a VAD (Voluntary Aid Detachment) hospital in Bishop's Stortford on Westfield Road and women worked at all the local shops, including the International Stores, a fact they were proud to advertise in the *Herts and Essex Observer*.[4]

The role of working women during the conflict had a huge impact on future generations. It must have affected the passing of the Reform Act in 1918, for example, which gave the vote to women over 30 (but, to encompass returning service men, to all 21-year old men). Only in 1928, however, was the voting age reduced to 21 for everybody.

Left: Claypits Farm Dairy in 1916. The message on the reverse of this postcard explains how the sender (the girl holding the hen) is to carry out hospital work, the man in the milk-cart (from Sparrow's) has been called up and the 'armlet' girl next to her now does the dairy round. The older woman holds a wicker basket to collect eggs.

Photograph of the Bridge Street and Market Street crossroads in the 1930s.

PART IV

The interwar years:

George V – George VI

24. Taking flight: early flying

Mike James

Leading up to the two World Wars, flight, unpowered in balloons then powered in aeroplanes, has a local history largely forgotten. Stansted Airport so close by is a reminder of the huge impact the airborne military had locally.

Powered flying was fraught with danger: near the Main Gate of Kew Gardens a notice beside an impressive Corsican Pine tree tells how a plane collided with it in the 1900s. Flying visitations in our locality included:

- On 8 June 1912, less than nine years after the Wright brothers' inaugural flight, crowds filled the streets at Epping to see four aircraft in the *Flying Derby* race fly over.

- Powered flight as a war-weapon was not far behind, and the extraordinary exploits and courage of Albert Ball are referred to on p72.

- In 1919 Captain Barratt (of Bishop's Stortford, second surviving son of A.S. Barratt) with No. 120 Squadron, flew for the Air Ministry a twin-engine, 3-seater, 420 H.P. DH10 aircraft non-stop, overnight, between Folkestone and Cologne (300 miles, averaging 100 mph against a head wind). In March-April, the squadron had carried 1634 bags of mail in 289 flights, losing only 10 days through adverse weather.

- Others too were able to make use of their wartime flying experience: In 1921 Frank Neale (late Royal Flying Corps – forerunner of the Royal Air Force) provided trips in a 3-seater Avro (*page opposite left*). His business was probably lucrative: he had already carried more than 5000 passengers on such trips in the UK.

- In 1924 glider trials from a launching carriage were held at Featherbys Ltd (later Millars), which in the First World War had manufactured munitions. And a twin-engined Vickers biplane crashed in Birchanger Wood: the pilot fortunately escaped.

- In 1932 Major Tommy Batman and John Rogers provided a flying display and pleasure flights at the Beldams Lane flying field, Bishop's Stortford, in a 40 HP Klemm monoplane.

In the Second World War, the flat farmland in our region provided ground for many airfields, including, locally, at Sawbridgeworth (a well-established pre-war airfield near Allen's Green in use constantly since 1940), Hunsdon (from May 1941), Great Dunmow (Little Easton, from July 1943) and, of course, Stansted (*see page 98*).

However, unpowered balloon flight occurred in England more than two centuries before powered flight began. On Wednesday 15 September 1784, 25-year old Vincent Lunardi took off from the grounds of the Honourable Artillery Company in London. His balloon was made of oiled silk in different colours and hydrogen-filled (*photograph opposite*). He waved flags to show he was really on board. Several gentlemen on horseback or foot followed his flight, which took 2¼ hours to cover 36 miles. Lunardi landed twice: once at South Mimms, where he set down the cat he had taken with him, which was suffering from cold; then, having jettisoned almost everything to regain height, at Standon. A stone (*top right*) still marks the landing spot.

By Victorian times the technology had advanced: In May 1883 the balloon of

FLYING!

(FOR TWO WEEKS ONLY).

Come and experience the joys of Flying on an

AVRO 3-SEATER

With

FRANK NEALE,

Of EPPING, late R.F.C. and R.A.F.,

At

BRAZIER'S MEADOW,

HALLINGBURY ROAD,

BISHOP'S STORTFORD

Flying from 10.30 till Dusk from **12/6** Flying Daily on and after Saturday, Jan. 22nd.

Above: Frank Neale's advert (*Herts and Essex Observer* 29 Jan 1921); an accompanying article indicates more than 100 passengers were taken up and the landings were reportedly very smooth! A Mr Brazier was a passenger, but whether that was Joe Brazier (not a small man) is unclear.

Walter Powell M.P. (who was carried out to sea in a balloon to his death), landed in Sadricks Field, Thorley: it was soon packed up and the occupants caught the last train at 8.57 p.m.

In 1897 Stortford crowds flocked to see a balloonist, Professor Fleet, arranged by Sir John Barker, perform his 18th parachute jump: the entrance fee went to the Rye Street Hospital. Dare-devil parachute performances were smash hits at this time – sometimes literally. Some on-site construction was required: A 35ft-long enclosed trench was dug with a tapered brick chimney at its end; a small fire provided the uplift: the balloon was placed over the chimney and took 20 minutes to fill. His silk parachute stretched 40 ft across; the balloon weighed nine cwt (457 kg) and took 100 cubic feet (2.8 m^3) of hot air to inflate. He was suspended from it by a webbing seat. On reaching 12,100 ft he disconnected and dropped, the parachute opened and he landed safely at Bury Green, the balloon coming down in Plantains Wood.

Based on an article by Nancy Poole.[1]

Above: The stone at Standon Green that marks the landing of Lunardi's balloon flight of 1784.

Above: Lunardi's balloon, its oars and basket, shown engraved on a commemorative copper plate fixed to the monument at Standon (*top*).

25. Rayments forge: shoeing for a century

Mike James

Above: Rayment's forge after conversion for Thebus Engineers Ltd. James Privett's house (background *left*) still stands.

Credit: Paul Ailey, www.stortfordhistory.co.uk

Many readers will remember the forge, and some will recall Arthur and Sidney Rayment working there. It stood on the corner of Chantry Road and Hadham Road, probably from the early 1860s until 2004 when it was demolished to make way for flats (now Watsons Yard).

The smithy was probably first started by veterinary surgeons Thomas and Harriet Folks to improve their business.[1] They occupied the next-door property (now The Folly) and a large garden. Its location was perfect: the Thursday market overflowed the High Street, Bridge Street and North Street areas and occupied more space in 1858 when G.E. Sworder opened the cattle market at Northgate End. So the new smithy allowed clients to avoid the crowded town centre.

Thomas Folks died in 1861. The veterinary side of the Folks business went in quick succession to T.G. Webb, MRCVS, in May, and then George Waters, MRCVS, in October. Stephen Eaton (from Manuden) took over the shoeing side in September and thereafter advertised himself in Trade Directories as 'shoeing smith, Hadham Road'. Eaton was a 'whitesmith' living in South Street, shaping metals like tin and pewter that can be worked cold, so the smithy was a natural business expansion for him.

In early April 1869 he changed career and became a licensed victualler, moving his family to the Bakers Arms in Bayford, Herts.

James Privett took over. Privett, unlike Eaton, was not local. He originally came from a poor agricultural community in Cocking, West Sussex. He trained as a blacksmith under his uncle (the splendidly named Melancthon Blanchard) and married his uncle's daughter Eliza (from Blanchard's first marriage).

Why the move to Bishop's Stortford? The couple had no relations here; perhaps it was the clean air, its prosperity and its transport links? However he heard about it, he took over the smithy against any local

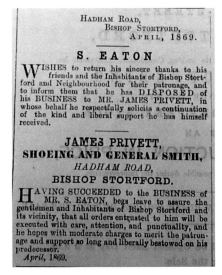

HADHAM ROAD,
BISHOP STORTFORD,
APRIL, 1869.

S. EATON

WISHES to return his sincere thanks to his friends and the Inhabitants of Bishop Stortford and Neighbourhood for their patronage, and to inform them that he has DISPOSED of his BUSINESS to MR. JAMES PRIVETT, in whose behalf he respectfully solicits a continuation of the kind and liberal support he has himself received.

JAMES PRIVETT,
SHOEING AND GENERAL SMITH,
HADHAM ROAD,
BISHOP STORTFORD.

HAVING SUCCEEDED to the BUSINESS of MR. S. EATON, begs leave to assure the gentlemen and Inhabitants of Bishop Stortford and its vicinity, that all orders entrusted to him will be executed with care, attention, and punctuality, and he hopes with moderate charges to merit the patronage and support so long and liberally bestowed on his predecessor.
April, 1869.

Above: Notice in the *Herts and Essex Observer* April 1869

competition and moved to Chantry Road where his first child was born in October 1869.

Privett enjoyed increasing prosperity. As his family grew he employed a nursemaid to help. To increase his income he bought properties he could let.

Arthur Rayment (from Great Waltham) was employed by Privett a few years later and eventually took over the smithy. In 1881, he lived in Rye Street with his young family. The *Herts and Essex Observer* of August 1889 records the terrible story of how Rayment's three year old daughter, Mina, was killed by a train as she ran after her elder brothers at the Parsonage railway crossing.

In 1904 Privett died and the smithy was sold to Sir Walter Gilbey for £530 (£45,000 today).[2] Gilbey's estate was later auctioned and the forge was bought by its then tenant,

Arthur C. Rayment, for £260 in 1917.[3]

Rayment, his son Arthur C., then his grandsons Arthur and Sidney, worked the smithy until it closed when Arthur and Sidney retired in the early 1970s. Thebus Engineers Ltd subsequently occupied the building some 110 years after the smithy first opened.

Above: Rayment's forge in action.

Above: Rayment's forge, 1956. Hubert Williams's painting from the Museum's collection shows the forge interior with Arthur C. Rayment's sons, Arthur (foreground) and Sidney.

26. Bishop's Stortford: philanthropy in the community

Mike James

In a report by the Charities Aid Foundation in 2010 the UK came joint eighth of 153 countries for charitable acts.[1]

Arguably, the Gilbey family were the greatest Bishop's Stortford benefactors of the Victorian-Edwardian period. Sir Walter Gilbey (1831–1914) and his brother Alfred (1833–79) became immensely wealthy by importing Cape wine and then developing a system of retailers to sell their wares. Sir Walter and his son Tresham (1862–1947), who married the only daughter of the Kensington department store magnate (and Stortford resident) Sir John Barker, came to own considerable property around Stortford. Plaques still commemorate the Gilbey's gifts (*photograph right*): in Cricketfield Lane (the Rugby Club, the tennis courts, cricket and playing fields), Bridge Street (at the Jackson Square entrance where the Town Mill stood, *see page 107*) and South Street (King's Cottages).

Bishop's Stortford Museum retains the Donors Board from the Rye Street Hospital. It records, from its inception in 1894 until 1942, 109 donations. Thirteen uncosted gifts include land (all from the Gilbeys), construction (by the Frere family, John Barker and

Above: Plaque commemorating Tresham Gilbey, a generous donor to the town of Bishop's Stortford.

other locals), furnishings and equipment (public subscriptions and individual donations). A total of £66,192 was additionally raised (£6.1M today): Gilbey family connections provided 45% while public fundraising contributed 12%. Most individual donations were under £120 (£11,000 today, still a sizeable sum).

Another popular and generous personality was Joe Brazier (1873–1948) who did much for Stortford, providing for the Football Club's Rhodes Avenue site in 1919 and gifting land to the town, including Sworders Field and establishing the Brazier Trust in 1928.[2] He was a JP and Chairman of the Bishop's Stortford Urban District Council. He managed both the George Hotel and the Chequers.

The postcard shown on the opposite page shows J. Kynnersley Kirby's painting of Joe Brazier *The Landlord of the Chequers*. It was exhibited at the Royal Academy in 1931 and was an instant hit. Brazier became a national celebrity. He paid Kirby £75 for it and then charged 6d to view it at the Chequers, the money going to the Rye Street Hospital fund. Brazier commented: "So it will do somebody a bit of good, won't it?".

With thanks to Sarah Turner.[3]

Right: On the reverse of this postcard, from the Museum's collection, is printed the message 'When passing through Bishop's Stortford, England, stop and see The Famous Academy Picture of Joe Brazier "The Landlord of the Chequers" and his dog "Pat.'.

27. The two-wheeler dealers of South Street

Mike James

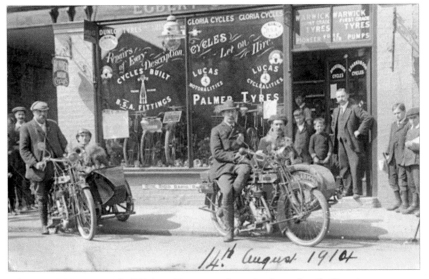

Above: 1914 postcard of Egbert Spearman's cycle shop, South Street.

The premises at 72 South Street (now Barnes Carpets) for many decades supplied the needs of Stortford's two-wheeled personal transport revolution. It witnessed a huge change, the end of horse power, in existence for millennia previously.

The postcard above captures the business's essence. Spearman had advertised as early as 1904 in the *Herts and Essex Observer*, as 'Cycle & Motor Agent', selling ladies' and gents' ten-guinea bicycles for £8 17s

6d – 15% off! The card above was posted on 28 August 1914, just 24 days after Britain declared war on Germany. Mr Spearman himself, with appropriate handle-bar moustache, stands in the doorway. The card may simply have been designed to promote Mr Spearman's shop, but it could also have promoted motorcycles for the war effort (see the article about Albert Ball, *pages 72-73*).

In 1918 he employed Alfred Tucker

(14), as a mechanic. Tucker stayed through all the business's transitions.

In the 1920s George E. Green took over (*photograph opposite*), repairing motorbikes and cars, and according to the shop sign, selling wireless receivers. It was the first business in Stortford to sell petrol (Shell) – the hose swung out over the pavement for customers parked outside.

Bill Thomas, with a partner also called Thomas but unrelated, acquired the business in 1927, becoming 'Thomas Brothers', although the partner soon departed.

At this time the mechanic, Tucker, was also a part-time fireman at the fire station further up South Street (now Boots Opticians). During the Second World War when the business collapsed, Tucker became a fulltime fireman (like his father).

Bill Thomas worked away in engineering and Bill's son Bernard joined the tank regiment. Bill's wife and mother lived over the shop, his mother storing locals' bicycles (2d each) neatly ordered in the rear yard, while customers shopped or visited the nearby cinema.

In October 1945 Alfred Tucker took over the business. Bernard Thomas emigrated to Toronto in 1952, to become a Chartered Engineer, his parents following later. Tucker, his brother Ernie and Wally Clayden (newly demobbed from active service) expanded Thomas Brothers post-war as motorised two-wheel transport increased. In 1956 they obtained the Lambretta scooter dealership (*photograph below right*), and the business flourished, attracting for the first time female clientele.

In 1957 Tucker died suddenly and his son Norman took over the business. Capturing the Honda agency in 1961 accelerated business further and it roared away in 1970 when they opened a new Suzuki dealership in Harlow to supply the town's expanding workforce.

In October 1970 Norman bought the shop next door (now Delicious Tea Rooms). The buildings were connected and 'Thomas Toys' opened: Norman sold toys from one side to the children of his motorcycle customers from the other. Increasing affluence meant that four-wheeled vehicles became more dominant than two; so Norman closed Thomas Brothers in 1985, nearly a century after the first two-wheeler dealer came to South Street.

With thanks to Norman Tucker.

Above: The business in the 1920s, when it was owned by George Green.

Above: Were you a Stortford Mod? Thomas Brothers after acquiring the Lambretta scooter dealership in 1957.

Photo credits for this article: Norman Tucker.

28. The last mansion in South Street

Mike James

The character of Bishop's Stortford's South Street has changed greatly over the last two centuries, much more than North Street. Early censuses show that South Street contained many residences, of town magnates as well as ordinary people.[1]

The proximity of the Stort Navigation and the railway, however, meant busy shops with living quarters above, warehouses and business premises took over from residences.

The last South Street mansion (*photograph opposite*) was demolished in 1937. It was a handsome, three storey red-brick building; for many years it accommodated the Bishop's Stortford Working Men's Club. Formerly, it was the residence of Frederick John Nash (1776–1854), modestly described as a 'common brewer' in the 1841 Census; in fact a wealthy partner of Hawkes & Co. the brewers of Water Lane. Reginald Jennings, a wealthy Maltster, lived in the Jacobean-style, pargetted house next door.[2]

Nash owned much of the land behind these properties bounded by Apton Road and Newtown Road, including a large garden and fields. His son, Jones Gifford Nash, also a brewery partner, owned a house across South Street known in the early 20th century as 'Miss Nash's house'. Another son, Frederick Woodham Nash (graduate of Felsted School, Cambridge University, and a barrister), owned Sion House in Birchanger, which still stands.

Left: This photograph shows the variety of purposes buildings were put to in South Street. The working men's club is on the far right of the picture, with notice boards outside; next to this is the Literary Institute, formerly R. Jenning's home. Beyond it is W.J. Skelton's bedding shop, and beyond that is a warehouse.

F.J. Nash's life had links to a forgotten era when hunting rights were held by the Lord of the Manor. In January 1814 he bought the hawking, hunting, fowling and fishing rights of the Manor of Stortford from the Bishop of London for seven years. The fee was 6d (2½p), two braces of hares and partridges and one brace of pheasants, to be paid to the Bishop annually. The Bishop also gave him the full power and authority to prohibit all other persons from hunting, including arresting and imprisoning them.[3]

The photographs (*right*) show the Working Men's Club, F.J. Nash's former residence, shortly before its demolition and relocation to South Road (now Bishop's Stortford Social Club). The land behind housed the 'Great Hall', a large meeting hall and venue of many lectures and entertainments. Today, a building containing the Edinburgh Woollen Mill and other shops stands there.

The older photograph (*page opposite*) shows other houses that stood next door (c. 1880). In the photograph they look shabby, but they had high status in their day.

Above: The Working Men's Club, formerly F.J. Nash's residence, shortly before demolition in 1937.

Above: South Street today from the same vantage point.

29. The weekend that set the town on fire

Mike James

The sombre picture on page 94 shows the Beech Flour Mill, built in 1882 in Dane Street, Bishop's Stortford, in flames at 3.00 a.m. on Saturday 22 June 1935.

The fire was an impressive sight: the Victorian design of the building and its tall chimney are clearly illuminated as the flames light the sky and are reflected in the river. The replacement building (*page opposite*), photographed from the same point on Station Road bridge some 20 years later, to some looks considerably uglier. The sign on the silo advertises '*Manufacturers, Cattle, Pig and Poultry Foods*'.

The Mill fire was a sensation in its own right, but especially because it immediately followed the huge fire that engulfed All Saints Church at Hockerill, starting only 15 hours previously. The Stortford, Stansted and Sawbridgeworth fire brigades were called but could not prevent the Church being totally gutted. The firemen bravely contended with smoke, molten lead, falling masonry and timber, and low water pressure. Injuries were, fortunately, not serious.

Above: Page reporting the fires: the *Herts and Essex Observer* 29 June 1935.

At the Mill fire Mr C.H. Edwards, the Mill owner, was asked by Stortford Brigade's Chief Officer Markwell, newly returned from the Church fire, to call out the Stansted and Sawbridgeworth brigades once again. They saved some of the Mill buildings and prevented the fire spreading to local houses. Both fires attracted large audiences.

The *Herts and Essex Observer* ran splash articles on Saturday 29 June (*photograph left*) including, uniquely, no less than eleven photos of the devastation, including the Museum's photograph (*page 94*). The dramas are recounted in the paper in great detail. Perhaps surprisingly, there seems to have been no suspicion of arson, even though in a small note the *Herts and Essex Observer* reported that a third fire, quickly extinguished, was discovered under the stairs at the Council Offices in the Causeway on the Friday morning.

Since photographs in the *Herts and Essex Observer* were then very unusual, the editorial staff perhaps went to Fleet Street for publishing assistance. The articles on the two

disasters were printed back to back. The Mill fire photo was taken by Ernest Williams, who ran a photographers business at 26 South Street. The *Herts and Essex Observer* probably had no photographer of its own, so perhaps most of the photos were by him.

Ernest Williams' former shop was recently taken over by the shop *East*. The building was extensively renovated, revealing the photographer's original shop sign behind the fascia, preserving another piece of history for the town.

With thanks to Sarah Turner.

Above: Photograph of the grain silo that replaced the original Victorian building after the fire, taken from the same spot on the Station Road Bridge.

Left: This picture shows the Beech Flour Mill in flames at 3.00 a.m. on Saturday 22 June 1935, photographed by Ernest Williams from Station Road Bridge.

Right: This atmospheric image of a fireman in the remains of All Saints Church presages similar images of the Blitz in the war to come.

"Never in the field of human conflict was so much owed by so many to so few"
The Prime Minister, August, 1940.

THE ROYAL AIR FORCE PILOTS AND CREWS FUND

THE FUND FOR "THE FEW"

Appeal by The Auctioneers' and Estate Agents' Institute
under the auspices of the Air Council.
IN CONNECTION WITH THE R.A.F. BENEVOLENT FUND.

HAVE YOU REMEMBERED TO SEND IN YOUR SAMPLES AND SEPARATE SCHEDULE?

Judges May Require Quality of Exhibits.
The Fund Requires NUMBER of Exhibits.

This form to be returned to G. E. SWORDER & SONS, BISHOP'S STORTFORD (Hon. Auctioneers for the Sale), on or before WEDNESDAY, DECEMBER 9th, 1942.

Bishop's Stortford
Christmas Fat Stock Show and Sale

To be held in the CATTLE MARKET, in aid of the above Fund
on THURSDAY, DECEMBER 17th, 1942,

With the Support of the Bishop's Stortford and Stansted Branches of the N.F.U.
President Major M. E. Barclay, J.P., M.F.H.

Fundraising sale by Sworders, Christmas 1942. Apart from livestock and miscellaneous goods, sale classes which won prizes included 'The best baconer' and 'The best Christmas Dinner (collection), including a brace of pheasants'.

PART V

The Second World War

30. Developing Stansted Airport

Mike James

Above: Job well done: the US army engineers who built Stansted airfield, with B–26 bombers in the background. Image courtesy of Ken Reed.

John Hamlin's 1997 book about the development of Stansted Airport[1] is fascinating: The wartime airfield was built from scratch by the 817th (replaced from May 1943 by the 825th) Engineer Aviation Battalion, US Army. They had arrived by ship, bringing their construction equipment with them. Construction started in July 1942, and was completed in February 1944, although aircraft began landing there from July 1943. For its time, it was massive. The runways were in a classical 'A' shape to cater for different wind directions. The longest was 6000 ft [1.83 km] and is the basis of today's runway. There were 15 'spectacle'-shaped hardstands for parking aircraft, an extensive bomb store, workshops, control tower and hangars for aircraft assembly.

There were dispersed sites for administration (comprising operations rooms, crew briefing, bomb-sight repair); domestic sites (staff quarters, barracks, latrines, ablutions); communal sites (ration and grocery store, tailor, barber, gym, squash court); mess rooms (a dining room for 800 airmen, officers and sergeants messes, showers and boiler house); as well as sick quarters, with a 22-bed hospital, dental surgery, mortuary and ambulance garage. Railway sidings at Stansted station were built to serve the airfield.

The site was designated USAAF Station 169, and assigned to the US 9th Air Force (motto: 'We win or die'). Aircraft arrived there from the USA by a circuitous route: USA to Puerto Rico, across the South Atlantic to Cornwall, and thence to Stansted. Their main purpose was major servicing and repair of B-26 Marauder bombers, which flew on raids over Europe from March 1944 leading up to D-Day, when 56 Stansted aircraft took part on the morning of 6th June alone. Altogether, in just seven months, 146 missions were flown, dropping 7,740 tons of bombs. But to win, aircraft were lost and men died.

The USAAF returned again in September 1953 to extend the main runway to 10,000 ft (3.05 km), its present length.

Apart from planes, the wartime impact of the US Engineers and Air Force was social too. Hamlin reports that as early as August 1942 a social evening and dance organised at Long's Restaurant in North Street was by invitation only because of demand. A USAAF band played, speeches of welcome were made and acknowledged. It was a great success. Saturday night dances at Long's became regular events, no doubt recalled by some readers.

After September 1944, the success of the Allied invasion meant that the airfield performed a holding and preparation function for new aircraft before their onward journey to more forward combat bases in Europe.

Stansted's civilian operations began towards the end of 1946 when London Aero & Motor Services Ltd (LAMS) bought surplus Halifax bombers to carry long-distance freight. The company took off and the rest, as they say, is history (and can be read in Hamlin's book).

GLAD TO SEE YOU, AMERICA !

Already the American uniform is a familiar sight in our streets. The men now among us are the vanguard of a vast army coming to aid in the restoration of liberty to the enslaved lands.

To these American boys Britain is a foreign land. Many of our customs and habits will be very strange. There are differences in national temperament that may lead to misunderstanding.

In dealing with our other allies we instinctively make allowances for such differences. Just because we start with a feeling of kinship and because we share the same language we are apt to be less understanding when we meet an American.

There is a deep welcome in our hearts for these friends and allies and there will be a widespread readiness to do all we can to make them feel at home.

As comrades now in winning the war and as comrades in building a better world to-morrow, we offer them a friendly greeting and a warm welcome.

Above: Herts and Essex Observer 1 August 1941. This editorial is just one of many articles and letters in the *Herts and Essex Observer* from 1941; it reports how Bishop's Stortford should adapt to the arrival of the American soldiers.

31. Memories of the Second World War

Alex Andrijevic

Bishop's Stortford Museum has been collecting memories as part of its ongoing Oral History project. Historical information about individuals, important events or reminiscences of everyday life have been recorded and these memories are to be preserved as an oral record for future generations. A significant challenge is often to edit the interviews afterwards so they are succinct without losing content. John Griggs and Ken Reed, from opposite ends of the town, shared their memories for the project.

Ken Reed was born and lived in Middle Row, New Town, Bishop's Stortford. He remembers the preparations for war being made in 1938. An air raid shelter was built at the rear of Flinn's Malting (now Coopers). Books were on sale with instructions of what to do in case of a raid and how to build a shelter indoors. Like many people, his first recollection of the war itself was listening to the radio broadcast by Neville Chamberlain (the Prime Minister) announcing that Great Britain was at war with Germany. He was sitting on his mother's lap in the kitchen, surrounded by the whole family.

Ken recalls that Bishop's Stortford suffered relatively few bombing raids. On a memorable occasion, one morning about 10 a.m. while at school at St Michaels, Apton Road (now the site of Apton Road car park) Ken heard the sound of an aircraft diving. He looked across Portland Road and saw a Junkers JU 88 bomber releasing its bombs. He ran to tell the headmaster (who was mixing powdered milk for the children's break). He got them all against the wall for cover, from where Ken had a good view of a Hurricane fighter attacking the JU 88: both were flying very low over the town. The bombs dropped by this aircraft landed near Bishop's Stortford Golf Club. Ken counted four bombs. Both Ken and John Griggs recall the curious moaning sound German bombers made. John, like most children during the war, had a book that identified British and German aircraft.

There were many aircraft crashes around the area and in the early days Ken would go after souvenirs, looking for shrapnel. Later there was so much that he didn't bother anymore.

AIR RAIDS.

IMPORTANT.

If the Warning Siren is sounded.

If you hear gunfire or bombs dropped in or near Bishop's Stortford.

1. You **must** keep inside your house. **Don't** go into the streets. The streets will be dangerous and the work of the fire brigade and A.R.P. services must not be hindered.

2. **Don't** leave your house until the "All Clear" is sounded unless it is on fire or the police tell you to leave.

3. Do **at once** what the police and wardens tell you.

4. Keep calm.

THE COUNCIL HOUSE,
BISHOP'S STORTFORD.

Above: Air raids and what to do. Finally, the advice is 'Keep calm'.

John Griggs, six months older than Ken, remembers what he recalls as the most serious bombing that took place, at Hockerill Teacher Training College (now Hockerill Anglo-European College), only 100 yards from his home. Three bombs were dropped that night: one landed in the middle of Dunmow Road near the College; one hit the College, collapsing a dormitory and blowing out the wall of another; and one hit the bank of the River Stort near Southmill Lock.

John's father was a member of the Air Raid Precaution Unit and on duty that night. John remembers his father telling him how three girls had died at the school during the bombing. They had broken the rules and hidden from the person in charge and had not gone to the shelters. Only later, after the all-clear, were their voices heard calling from beneath the rubble, but by the time rescuers got to them they had suffocated.

There were air-raid shelters for homes of two designs: Morrison and Anderson, named after Government Ministers of the time. Anderson shelters were provided for assembly in the garden; Morrison shelters were erected indoors. It seems people had their preferences according to circumstance: Ken's father was provided with a Morrison shelter but he returned it because it took up too much space. Made of steel it looked like a table with a large steel sheet on top. As Ken recalls it looked like a cage but no doubt saved lives. John's father was a gardener; he refused to lose his garden to the Anderson shelter, so had a Morrison shelter instead. It was delivered in parts to be assembled in a downstairs room.

Ken Reed and John Griggs have lived in Bishop's Stortford most of their lives, but it was at the Bishop's Stortford Museum that they first met, only a few years ago, to share their memories.

With thanks to Ken Reed and John Griggs.

Above: Wings for Victory leaflet. This national campaign to help fund Spitfire planes was taken up with enthusiasm by the residents of Bishop's Stortford.

A child's 'Mickey Mouse' gas mask

In the Second World War the entire population was issued with gas masks because of the fear that the enemy would drop poison gas. The horror of poison gas use from the First World War remained very strong. In an attempt to make such things more acceptable, masks of a smaller size, for children under five years, were made in red and blue and were, accordingly, known as 'Mickey Mouse' masks.

Air intake was through the blue activated-charcoal filter at the bottom; exhalation was via the flat, red nose-piece which acted as a non-return valve (and could be made to whistle).

Much attention was paid to warning the population about the risks of gas, what to do in the event of an attack, and the importance of keeping your gas mask about you at all times, especially during air raids.

Coronation mug, 1953.

PART VI

The new Elizabethans

32. Where is the bridge in Bridge Street?

Mike James

Above: Photograph of Mill Bridge and the Old Town Mill c. 1890.

Some readers will remember the bridge (*photograph above*) in Bridge Street before Stortford was redeveloped in the late 1960s.

The layout of UK towns and roads had changed little in the previous century, but post-war prosperity had increased traffic congestion hugely. In 1963 a Report, *Traffic in Towns,*[1] proposed urban redevelopment that would separate pedestrians from traffic. The result was massive town centre reconstruction throughout the country. In Stortford the proposals were radical: diversion of the river, but also clearance of much of the historic centre – the Corn Exchange was only saved following an appeal in 1967.

Mill Bridge stood opposite the modern entrance to Jackson Square where the pedestrian crossing now is. A plaque recalling the Mill is located nearby (*photograph far right*).

The picture (*left*), taken in the late 1890s, looks from Flinn's yard (now Cooper's, previously Maslen's) towards the Bridge. The Old Town Mill is the weather-boarded building (demolished 1899) on the other side of Bridge Street, where Photosound and Mamdani Opticians now are. On the bridge, a post boy on his bicycle has stopped to watch the photographer.

The locations of the bridge and Bridge Street are likely ancient thoroughfares: J.L. Glasscock, builder and town historian who photographed the Town Mill in 1890, found the original road surface 4½ feet below Water Lane by the Star Inn when workers were installing a drain.[2]

The picture below looks north from Mill Bridge towards the rear buildings and yard of what is now Coopers and the former maltster's house. The Stort broadened out here to form the mill pool that powered the mill wheel. Redevelopment filled in the river bed to extend Flinn's yard and create Old River Lane and the Waitrose car park. Walking along the pavement next to

Above: This view of the Stort from Mill Bridge was published as a postcard and posted in 1916. The town meads, to the right, were frequently flooded.

Coopers (in the middle of the river, as it were) you may imagine how it looked in the 1840s, where beyond Flinn's Maltings were private gardens, maltings, a tannery and then Hawkes & Co.'s brewery (where Waitrose is now); an area that was possibly included within the original Anglo-Saxon town.

The picture below left, taken in about 1967, shows the river downstream from the Mill. Flinn's roof is just visible beyond the sluice (and bridge) where the mill wheel once turned. During redevelopment, the river was rerouted around the Castle to join the Stort Navigation's Hockerill Cut, and culverted under Old River Lane. Mill

Bridge, the Mill's spillway and all but a stub of the Terminus Basin have vanished beneath Jackson Square.

Above: Photograph c. 1967 looking north across Terminal Basin and Mill Bridge towards the maltings buildings which now house Coopers.

Above: Photographs showing the barely decipherable plaque which marks the site of the Town Mill. It reads 'Site of the Old Town Mill. Given to the Town by Sir Walter Gilbey Bart 1911'.

33. Preserving Stortford's ancient woodland

Mike James

As the population increases, towns inevitably expand. Stortford's 'New Town' to the south of Newtown Rd expanded into neighbouring meadows in the early 19th century to provide living space, just as Thorley Park and St Michael's Mead have today and plans for Dane O'Coys Road will tomorrow. Old photographs and maps give a sense of roads being built and streets widened as Stortford's prosperity increased. The surrounding countryside also provides evidence of our past, for example Birchanger Wood is an important vestige of ancient woodland.

In the Domesday Book[1] (a tax assessment for King William I in 1086) 'Storteford' was rated poorer than 'Sabrixteworde' (Sawbridgeworth), or Brent Pelham, the Hadhams, Thorley or Albury (but while the others had declined under the Conqueror, Stortford's value had increased). 'Storteford' had fewer farmer/workers than 'Sabrixteworde' (31 versus 164) but, exceptionally, woods to feed 300 hogs – an important staple then. Hoggets Wood, Hoggets Wood Field, Hoggets Wood Pasture (all by Dane O'Coys Road), and Hoggets Mead (north of Maze Green Rd) all recall this economy. Birchanger Wood was part of a larger Manor that fed 100 hogs; now it covers just 69 acres. It was encroached by the post-war Parsonage Lane development, but was fortunately saved by Council purchase.

The Wood forms a complex ecology: London clay supports oak, hornbeam and birch; chalk subsoils support ash, maple and hazel. Apart from sustaining pigs, it was coppiced to provide a renewable timber source for everyday needs. Trees were cut back to a low trunk ('stool'), stimulating vigorous lateral regrowth for cutting a few years later. Coppicing trees in rotation allows annual harvesting throughout the wood. As coppicing recurs stools increase in diameter; the central stool may even disappear with age. Some good examples are also found in Hatfield Forest.

Tree species have preferred uses: ash and hazel for green bowls and stools; birch for besoms, charcoal and gunpowder; chestnut for fencing; hornbeam for firewood and the teeth of wind- and watermill gears; oak for building and furniture; sycamore and maple for churns. Sweet chestnut (a Roman introduction) and hazel are food crops too. All these species are found in Birchanger Wood, tending to be located together, evidence of the bodgers' industry.

Trees were last coppiced there around 1937, but the existence of stools about 2m in diameter and numerous flora indicate its longevity. Carpets of spring-flowering species have developed, including wood anemone, bluebell, cowslip and primrose. But new growth is enjoyed too by deer, rabbit and squirrel – in former times all would have been hunted for the pot and to protect the crop. Another current threat is vandalism, which the Birchanger Wood Trust is seeking to minimise through education. Enjoy their website,[2] stroll the new footpaths and smell the history.

With thanks to Pat Forrest.

Changing seasons in Birchanger Wood. *Top left*: Large coppice stool (left) and new path in March. *Left*: A wonderful carpet of wood anemones in April. *Above*: Birch and coppiced hornbeam in November.

Credit: Photographs lower left and top right courtesy of Dr Roger Wilmot:

www.pbase.com/rogerwilmot/birchanger.

34. Remembering royal events ...

Museum staff and volunteers

20 November 1947: I was 2½ at the time that the Queen, then Princess Elizabeth, married Philip Mountbatten; I remember listening to the event, which was broadcast on the radio, with my mother.'

'The Queen's Coronation in 1953 had a big impact on me. My parents bought our first television so we could watch it in our own home. Alas, being a very young lad I was so taken with the coach procession that I remember nothing of the coronation itself'

Silver Jubilee, 1977: 'We had lived in our street for several years before the Jubilee, but we knew only our immediate neighbours at all well. When Jubilee day arrived, my wife (a teacher who could keep good order!) helped at the children's street party, organised by the mums in the afternoon. In the evening there was a party for the adults. We did not know the hosts, and they did not know us. It turned out the husband thought we were interlopers and didn't live in the street at all! We assumed, because we didn't recognise them either, they had only recently moved in. We were mutually amazed when we discovered that we had all resided in the same street for more than half a decade.'

'For the Jubilee at school the children made paintings of the Queen and red, white and blue bunting. We made a large Union Jack of tissue paper, showing how the three national flags combined.'

'Perhaps my first memory – being taken to the big house in Manuden, Mrs Prior's house, and being given a souvenir jubilee mug from the boot of someone's car.'

'In the Jubilee in 1977, I was staying with my grandparents who lived on the north coast of Cornwall. There was a village fete arranged in a field that sloped down to the sea; it was a hot sunny day.'

Elizabeth II's Golden Jubilee in 2002: 'I had to make a King costume for my 5-year old son, who doesn't like dressing up, so that he could go to the school party. I sewed a long piece of gold ribbon to a red headscarf to use as a cloak and between us we made a gold cardboard crown.'

'Cecil Close celebrated the Queen's Golden Jubilee by closing the road and holding a barbecue. It was a beautiful day and the residents all contributed to the celebrations. Houses had bunting and there were tables in the middle of the road.'

2011: 'Cecil Close also celebrated the Royal Wedding in April with a barbecue. However, as it was April we had a marquee in one of the back gardens – and a good time was had by all.'

Notes

Part I. Jubilees and royal visits

1. Queen Victoria's Jubilees

1. Details from *Queen Victoria's Jubilees, Bishop's Stortford 1887 & 1897*. H Copley & Co.'s Diamond Jubilee Year Book, Almanack, Directory and Diary for 1898.

2. King Edward VII: celebrations and visitation

1. Details like this can be seen in the photographs in the Museum's collection.

2. *Herts and Essex Observer*, 4 November 1905.

3. Celebrations for George V and George VI

1. Programme of Proceedings Silver Jubilee Celebrations HM King George V, 6 May 1935.

2. Programme of Proceeding for Coronation celebrations, 12 May 1937.

4. The new Elizabethan age

1. These and other details from *Bishop's Stortford Celebrations Souvenir Programme*: Coronation of HM Queen Elizabeth II, 2 June 1953.

Part II. The Victorians and Edwardians

5. Coach travel and Stortford's inns

1. Bibliography: Wright W.J.

2. Directory: *Essex, Herts and Middlesex*, J. Pigot & Co, London, September 1839. Facsimile edition. Bishop's Stortford Museum collection.

3. Bibliography: *Diary of Samuel Pepys*, Vol 2, p355 & 513-6.

4. Bibliography: Sanders H.I.

5. *Pepys paints colourful picture, Herts and Essex Observer,* 7 March 1991.

6. From *Supplement of Reserved Songs from Merry Drollery* (1661), courtesy Phil Gyford, www.pepysdiary.com/p/11686.php

6. Commerce wins over the old King's Head

1. ERO ref: A10663, Box 2; also HALS ref: Deeds 56513-15.

2. Now Lloyds TSB, Sidney Street, Cambridge; *Fosters'* (plural possessive because there were several Foster partners) remains carved over the entrance.

Notes

7. Fighting crime and the new model police station

1. Bibliography: Turner, Sarah.

2. Bishop's Stortford Museum police records.

3. HALS: British Schools Log Book ref HEd 1/85/7.

9. The astonishing story of John Dobede Fairman

1. *The Times* 16 June 1860; *London Gazette* 22 August 1862. The Times Archive and the London Gazette available online are searchable for information on military Commissions, bankruptcies, Government notices, etc, etc. See also HALS D/EX99/L1 which contains many documents about Fairman's bankruptcy.

2. These and other calculations were made using *Inflation: the value of the pound 1750-2002*, House of Commons research paper 03/82, 11 November 2003.

3. *The Times,* 4 April 1882.

4. Ancestry.co.uk searches provide considerable information about births, marriages, deaths and Census documents.

10. Chantry house and the man who built it.

1. The Gatehouse (next to *Aristocrat*) on Hadham Road is an older construction presumably originally leading to a contemporary building older than George Starkins' house of 1823-4.

2. Will of George Starkins' father (also called George) dated 30 October 1773. ERO ref: D/DBi T34 with additional documentation.

3. Pigot's Directory for Stortford references in 1824 'Chaplin Fred. tanner, near North-st'; in 1826-7 'Starking & Chaplin, tanners, North st'; in 1828 'Chaplin, tanner, North St'; in 1832 the Hertfordshire Directory references 'Starkins & Chaplin, Tanners, Water Lane'.

4. Essex Records Office (ERO) ref: D/DB T1673 provides the office copy of George Starkins' Will with the associated documentation. His Will and the associated map is also available from the National Archive online.

5. ERO ref: D/DMd/200-203 for the niece's and tenant's testimonies.

11. How local enterprise developed Bishop's Stortford

1. J.L. Glasscock's Ledger, Bishop's Stortford Museum BSM 268/2, pp176–184.

2. The Bishop's Stortford Water Act 1869 given Royal Assent 24 June 1869.

3. J.L. Glasscock, *Some Stortford Inns and Inn Signs. Herts and Essex Observer*, 8 November 1919.

4. J.L. Glasscock's Ledger, Bishop's Stortford Museum BSM 268/2, p164.

Notes

12. How housing development has changed its style

1. The 1832 Reform Act gave votes to freeholders owning land worth £2 a year (among other types of landholder), favouring the middle classes. The Chartist Movement sought from 1836 to provide greater rights for the working classes, including universal male suffrage. Petitions with many signatures were presented to Parliament in 1839, 1842 and then 1848, but were rejected amid riots in the industrialised towns. The importance of landholding to secure voting rights was thereby emphasised; the National Freehold Land Society was established in 1849 to facilitate land purchase for this purpose.

2. HALS holds several complex deeds about the Chantry Estate sale (e.g. D/EB1813/T1 and D/EL/T24), as well as Summers & Sworder's sale documents.

13. A Victorian 'Grand Design'

1. *Death of Mr G.E. Pritchett, Herts and Essex Observer* 2 March 1912, contains an extensive obituary.

2. Nancy Poole's sources are not always traceable and are simply repeated here.

3. HALS ref: D/ETe/D31 concerns the ownership of Beehive and Firtree cottages, Pleasant Road.

4. *Sale of antiquities at Oak Hall, Herts and Essex Observer*, 13 July 1912.

5. *Letter, Herts and Essex Observer*, 20 July 1912.

6. *Turning a dream into reality, Herts and Essex Observer*, 28 March 1991.

14. Selling your house in the 19th century

1. Tim Turner is gratefully acknowledged for sharing his researches into the history of Sworders.

15. Family life in the town centre

1. Ancestry.co.uk for access to census documents.

2. J.L. Glasscock's Ledger, Bishop's Stortford Museum BSM 268/2.

16. If you want to get ahead, get a servant!

1. Bibliography: May, Trevor, *Women at work,* Chapter 10.

2. A photo of a very similar shop appears in Violet Sparrow's *Bishop's Stortford, a Pictorial History* (Phillimore & Co, 1996, Fig. 52) but is most likely the sisters' shop in Lowestoft.

3. Census documents obtainable through Ancestry.co.uk.

Notes

17. Messrs Hawkes & Co. are proud to announce …

1. Bibliography: Whittaker, Allan.

2. 'Entire' appeared under the Hawkes name on the brewery's pub signs.

3. *Building is a special brew*, *Herts and Essex Observer,* 18 April 1991.

18. Cecil Rhodes and his portraits

1. Bibliography: Cole, Tennyson P: Chapter 20, p162. Bishop's Stortford Museum also holds a large Rhodes archive.

2. Bibliography: Campbell C, *et al.* p159.

19. Costumes—what's in *your* attic?

1. Sprecher, Danielle: *Advice and report on 1903 wedding dress*; Bishops Stortford Museum, 28 May 2010.

Part III. The First World War

20. Dad's Army 1914-18

1. For further details see Bibliography: Mitchinson, K.W.

2. These and other details are from the *Herts and Essex Observer* October — November 1914, and HALS ref: D/EX47/Z1-7 about the 1st Battalion Hertfordshire Regiment.

3. *Herts and Essex Observer,* November 1918.

21. Albert Ball, VC. A fighter pilot in Bishop's Stortford

1. These and other details are from several sources, including Wikipedia; see also Bibliography: Briscoe & Stannard; Bowyer C; also the Lenton (Nottinghamshire) Local History Society website www.lentontimes.co.uk.

2. *Herts and Essex Observer,* March 1915.

22. Oak Hall, the German prisoner of War camp

1. Many details from the *Herts and Essex Observer,* March 1918 – February 1919.

23. Women at war: the Land Army

1. The Women's Farm Competition was reported in the *Herts and Essex Observer* almost weekly from 23 June 1917 to 11 August 1917.

2. Pathe News – www.britishpathe.com – *The Harvesting Girls of Bishop's Stortford 1914-1918*.

3. *Herts and Essex Observer,* 6 March 1918.

4. *Herts and Essex Observer*, 19 August 1916.

Notes

Part IV. The Interwar years: George V – George VI

24. Taking flight: early flying

1. *Balloons to bombers*, *Herts and Essex Observer*, 4 April 1991; also see reports in this newspaper contemporary to the events.

25. Rayments forge: shoeing for a century

1.Notices in the *Herts and Essex Observer* of 1861 & 1869; trade directories (Bishop's Stortford Museum and HALS), census documents and other material from Ancestry.co.uk allow this history to be pieced together. The James Privett family tree is also available on Ancestry.co.uk.

2. The Gilbey Archive: *Properties* and *Cash Book*, Bishop's Stortford Museum.

3. HALS ref: D/EX546/B2, sale particulars of Gilbey Estate, 27 November 1917.

26. Bishop's Stortford: philanthropy in the community

1. See www.cafonline.org/press-office/press-releases.aspx p8: *World Giving Index launches*, 8 September 2010.

2. Registered charity no. 302336, Charity Commission website www.charity-commission.gov.uk.

3. We gratefully acknowledge Michael Belcher for the loan of his scrapbook compiled by Brazier: *The Landlord of the Chequers by J. Kinnersley Kirby, Royal Academy 1931*.

28. The last mansion in South Street

1. Bell Street in Sawbridgeworth still retains that mix of desirable housing, small shops, flats, sack hoists and pubs.

2. From census documents and the 1839 Bishop's Stortford Tithe Map and Award (HALS ref: DSA/4/21/1-2).

3. HALS ref: D/P21 29/30, 20 January 1814, from J.L. Glasscock's notes and transcripts of parish records.

Part V. The Second World War

30. Developing Stansted airport

1. Bibliography: Hamlin, John.

Part VI. The New Elizabethans

32. Where is the bridge in Bridge Street?

1. Wikipedia: *Traffic in towns*. Report by Prof Sir Colin Buchanan, HMSO, London, 1963.

2. J.L. Glassock's Ledger, Bishop's Stortford Museum BSM 268/2, p155.

Notes

33. Preserving Stortford's ancient woodland

1. Bibliography: Chauncy, Henry.
2. www.birchangerwoodtrust.org.

Bibliography

Bishop's Stortford: a short history; Bishop's Stortford & District Local History Society, Bishop's Stortford, 1984.

Bowyer C. *Albert Ball VC,* William Kimber & Co. London 1977.

Briscoe W.A. & Stannard H.R. *Captain Ball VC: the career of Flight Commander Ball VC, DSO.* Herbert Jenkins, London, 1918

Campbell C, James M, Reed P & Schwartz S: *The Art of William Nicholson.* Royal Academy of Arts, London 2004.

Chauncy, Henry: *The historical antiquities of Hertfordshire*; JM Mullinger, Bishop's Stortford, 1826.

Cole, Philip Tennyson: *Vanity varnished: reminiscences in many colours*; Hutchinson & Co. Ltd, London, 1931.

Hamlin, John: *The Stansted experience*; GMS Enterprises, Peterborough, 1997.

Mitchinson K.W. *Defending Albion: Britain's Home Army 1908-1919.* Palgrave Macmillan, Basingstoke, 2005.

May, Trevor: *An economic and social history of Britain 1760 – 1970.* Longman Group, Harlow, 1987.

Diary of Samuel Pepys, with notes by Richard Lord Braybrooke; Everyman's Library edition, JM Dent & Sons, London, 1917.

Sanders, Henry I.: *The Gilbey family.* In: *Local History Chronicles: Part 1*; Bishop's Stortford & District Local History Society, Bishop's Stortford, 2005.

Turner, Sarah: *the former police station, King Street, Watford.* Built Environment Advisory and Management Service, September 2006

Whittaker, Allan: *Brewers in Hertfordshire: a historical gazetteer*; Hertfordshire Publications, University of Hertfordshire, Hatfield, 2006.

Wright, W.J. *Taken on Trust: the roads of Bishop's Stortford.* In: *Local History Chronicles: Part 1*; Bishop's Stortford and District Local History Society, Bishop's Stortford, 2005.

Acknowledgements

The richness of these histories would have been impossible without the primary sources available in the collections of the Bishop's Stortford Museum itself; in Hertfordshire Archives and Local Studies, Hertford (HALS: www.hertsdirect.org); Cambridgeshire Archives and Local Studies, Cambridge (CALS: www.cambridgeshire.gov.uk/leisure/archives); the Essex Records Office, Chelmsford (ERO: www.seax.essexcc.gov.uk); the National Archives online (www.nationalarchives.gov.uk) and Ancestry.co.uk (www.ancestry.co.uk). We gratefully acknowledge the helpfulness and patience of Archive staff; also the staff and services of Bishop's Stortford Public Library where *The Times Archive* is available online. Paul Ailey provides the *Stortford History* website (www.stortfordhistory.co.uk); Bishop's Stortford & District Local History Society (BS&DLHS) has published several booklets about the locality, and its work over the years has contributed hugely to the Museum's archive.

Sarah Stephens Photography (www.sarahstephensphotography.co.uk) provided the photographs on pages 31, 35, 39, 41, 50, 51, 61, 66, 67, 77, 85 and 103; the objects photographed are all part of the Bishop's Stortford Museum collection. Historical photographs also originate from the Museum's collection, unless acknowledged differently. Many of the articles were written by Mike James, who helped design and edit the book with his co-authors' and two reviewers' help. Some of the articles were published in earlier form under the 'Nostalgia' banner in the *Herts and Essex Observer*: Thanks go to Paul Winspear (Editor) and Alex Day (then Deputy Editor) for accepting them, only slightly altered, and to article co-authors Alex Andrijevic (Museum Deputy Curator), Pat Forrest (Warden & Trustee, Birchanger Wood Trust), John Griggs (BS&DLHS), Norman Tucker (ex two-wheeler) and Dr Sarah Turner (Museum Curator). Nancy Poole also wrote nostalgia articles for the *Observer* (archived at HALS); some from 1991 have been adapted with due acknowledgement. Inaccuracies found in published articles have been corrected. Specific acknowledgements also occur in the relevant text.

Many thanks to Michael S. Brown (Museum volunteer) for his help. Thanks also to Wally Wright (BS&DLHS), Dorothy Pegrum, Mary and Theresa Cannon, Clive Kitchener (B.S. Social Club), Tim Turner (G.E. Sworder & Sons), Ken Reed, and all the Museum volunteers and staff for great discussions and for making volunteering at the Museum so interesting. Mike James is grateful to his wife Irene for her patience and editorial help during this production.

Finally, we particularly acknowledge the Nineveh Charitable Trust (reg. charity no. 256025) and grants from Cllr John Barfoot and Cllr Colin Woodward from the Hertfordshire County Council Locality Budget Scheme towards the publication costs of this book.

The *Nineveh Charitable Trust* supports a broad range of UK-based projects and activities of benefit to the General Public, with an emphasis on promoting a better understanding of the environment and countryside, whilst facilitating improved access, education and research. Visit www.ninevehtrust.org.uk for more about our aims and achievements.